10.60

JAMES B. WYNGAARDEN, M.D.
DEPARTMENT OF MEDICINE
DUKE UNIVERSITY MEDICAL CENTER
DURHAM, NORTH CAROLINA 27710

To Larry and Cleota Pugsley.

John A. Pugsley

COMMON SENSE

ECONOMICS

YOUR GUIDE
TO
FINANCIAL
INDEPENDENCE
IN THE
AGE OF INFLATION

The Common Sense Press, Santa Ana, California

Graphics and cover design by Peter Ragland.

Copyright © 1974 by John A. Pugsley.
Second printing, April, 1975

Library Congress Catalog Card Number: 74-24499

Manufactured in the United States of America.

FOREWORD

The book you are about to read is true. The subject covered affects your life directly and more profoundly than any other social phenomenon. There are many opinions as to the importance and correctness of economic actions; in the end there is only one truth, only one correct opinion. I firmly believe it is presented here.

I take no credit whatsoever for the discovery and development of the economic ideas encompassed in the doctrine of laissez-faire capitalism. I can only recognize and extend my thanks to those writers and lecturers who have, through their genius and skill, caused me to understand economic and social reality and enabled me to penetrate the morass of fallacious argument that comprises current economic and investment thinking.

Who should get the credit for the right thinking expressed in this book? In terms of the ideas about economics and government interference in the marketplace, probably Ludwig von Mises deserves the greatest amount of credit. He was a world renowned Austrian economist who started writing early in this century. Although I haven't read all his works, nor can I say that all my conclusions are direct derivations of his ideas, his thoughts certainly were the seeds that influenced subsequent writers who in turn influenced me. I'm certain he, in turn, would want to credit his teacher Eugen von Bohm-Bawerk who was the founder of the Austrian school of economics.

Both Murray Rothbard and Henry Hazlitt deserve star billing. Dr. Rothbard's book *America's Great Depression* was both shocking and exciting in its revelation of the causes of the economic debacle of the thirties. I have always been impressed by careful scholarship and adherence to scientific principles and Dr. Rothbard's book was a fine example of both.

Henry Hazlitt's little tome *Economics In One Lesson* should be required reading for all economists, politicians and businessmen around the world. In fact, it should be read by everyone. I probably never would have written this book but for his inspiration. Although I don't cite any of his other works, he's a prolific writer on the subject of economics and has devoted his life to purging the world of the black fog of Keynesianism.

One of the writers that Mr. Hazlitt gives credit to should also be mentioned, even though not specifically referenced in the text. That is Frederic Bastiat who wrote *The Law* way back in 1850. It is a masterpiece of timeless economic truth. Read it.

I warmly thank Thomas Paine for writing the original pamphlet *Common Sense* in 1776. Had all his thoughts and reasoning been followed, perhaps we would still be free today, and this book would not be necessary.

While giving credit, I shouldn't overlook those around me who offered the encouragement, advice and physical aid to bring this book into being. Winston Griepp, LLB, good friend and counsel, gave the original inspiration and continuing confidence to start and finish the task. Page Rank and Margaret Grahn offered both encouragement and financial assistance. I would also like to thank Mr. John P. Dye, with whom I associated for several years, for introducing me to the basics of life insurance, mutual funds, and the S4/B1 switching system discussed on page 148.

My staunchest supporter has been my wife, Gloria Terry. Her encouragement, as well as her help in editing the manuscript, was essential to the completion of the work.

Contents

INTRODUCTION

In the period from January 1, 1969 to January 1, 1975, five years, the following companies have come to public attention: United Professional Planning, Carriage Company, Groesbeck Company, Capital Concepts, Geotek, Mont Beef, Black Watch Farms, Natural Resources, King Resources, Urbanetics, Home Stake Production Company, Four Seasons Nursing Homes, Penn Central Railroad, Equity Funding, Lockheed Aircraft, United California Bank of Switzerland, Franklin Bank of New York, Herstatt Bank of Germany. What do they have in common? Failure, and along with it the loss of billions of dollars of investors' money. The stock market itself remains, even with inflation to buoy its value, at tens of billions less in value than at the beginning of the period. Even in what must be considered the most conservative of assets, bonds, we have witnessed profound losses as bond prices plummet in the face of rising interest rates. Since the days of the great depression, never have we witnessed such immense losses and never in such diverse and seemingly safe investments as the last five years.

Headlines in the financial press daily report the trembling in the financial markets as investors rush from the stock market to the precious metals, from the metals to bonds, from bonds back again to the stock market. Meanwhile, only with massive infusions of credit has the government been able to prevent a total flight of depositors from savings & loans, banks, and life insurance companies.

From every direction come cries of advice: buy gold, buy silver, buy Swiss francs, buy stocks, buy real estate, buy options. For every voice crying buy, another voice cries: don't buy, stay away, do the opposite. This is the climate in which you as an individual are living. Your goal is survival and the accumulation of enough wealth to provide for yourself when you no longer wish to, or are no longer able to work. The stark facts are that very few people in this country

are going to survive the financial and economic cataclysm
that will occur over the next decade.

Of those who do survive, a handfull will do it because of
sheer luck. They just happened to own the right asset at the
right time. The great majority of those who succeed
financially will do it because they understand the causes of
the economic turmoil, and by understanding the causes will
be able to predict the course of the events of the world. For
the great masses of investors, the next ten years will mean the
end of their wealth. They are the ones who will foolishly go
forward under the assumption that the future will be the
same as the past. They will continue their current high
standard of living and will maintain their same investment
patterns and strategies. They won't bother to try to
understand in any depth what is happening to cause these
turbulent financial markets; they'll move into the future
handling their money carelessly, without even an understanding of what money really is, and taking their investment
advice from salesmen who are themselves ignorant of the
underlying economic forces working in the marketplace.
They will fail financially, and that failure will sentence them
to lives of dependence on the charity of the state. Those who
succeed will do so against overwhelming odds, and they will
do so because they are consciously or unconsciously following the natural economic principles as outlined in this
book.

No one can afford to stop after this. It is nothing more
than a guidepost to direct you along the road to financial
independence. To succeed at accumulating wealth you must
study the subject thoroughly and deeply. You should read
every reference work cited, and many more that aren't. If you
think that it's too much trouble, then you're forgetting the
effort it takes you to earn money to start with. Can you
afford not to understand what it is once you've earned it, and
still expect to keep it? Gaining a fundamental knowledge of

economics and investments is the most important thing you can do for yourself in your lifetime. It's survival itself.

J.A.P.
Newport Beach, California
April, 1975

CHAPTER ONE

Money, Government, and You

WEALTH, THE ELUSIVE GOAL—

Two friends each decided to build a house. The first, Jones, started by giving a lot of thought to the type of house that he wanted. He made rough sketches, lists of features, and penciled out his estimate of costs; then went to an architect, and together they sketched out room dimensions and floor plans. When he was confident the architect knew what was wanted, he commissioned him to go forward and design the house. Drawing on his knowledge of local conditions, including building codes, weather, terrain, soil conditions, etc., the architect decided on the general structural components of the building. With his knowledge of engineering and building materials, he carefully designed the house down to the very last light-switch plate. Then he had another meeting with Jones, the design was confirmed, and final adjustments to the drawings were made. From there, a contractor was hired, plans filed and materials ordered. Inasmuch as the contractor and architects were honest, knowledgeable and industrious, the house turned out exactly as Jones had wanted.

Smith, Jones' friend, took a more direct approach to his house. Rather than spend time fooling around with plans (he was very busy with his business at the time), he simply went down to the lumber company, ordered what appeared to be ample quantities of two-by-fours, plywood, cement, paint

and plaster, and had them delivered to his lot. He arrived the
following morning, along with his brother (a garage mech-
anic) and his wife's uncle (a dentist), and they set to work.

Unfortunately, his relatives soon tired of helping, and he
found himself alone with the project. He hammered, sawed
and did his best to design the house as he went along,
occasionally cursing his lack of this or that material or
wondering what in the world to do next. Fortunately, he
could always call on his relatives for advice. (Although
neither of them had ever built a house, they were more than
willing to tell him how it should be done.) But, alas, the task
was too great. In the end, he never finished. The project, as
you can imagine, became an impossibility.

No one felt sorry for Smith, for everyone in the
neighborhood recognized that he was a fool. You can't build
a decent house without a lot of planning, and they pointed at
Jones' house as proof. The whole thing was obvious.

Now, compare the problem of doing a simple thing such as
building a house with the problem of becoming independently wealthy. Which would you say is easier? Almost
everyone lives in a house of some sort, and someone had to
build that house; so it might follow that home building is
relatively easy. But it's only easy if it's done *right*.

And independent wealth? How many people who work
for a living manage to accumulate enough wealth to become
financially independent? According to U.S. Government
statistics, only three people out of a hundred have enough
wealth to provide themselves with an income of three
thousand dollars a year at age 65. Why? Because they have all
approached building a fortune the same way Mr. Smith
approached building his house: without a design (goal),
without knowledge of building materials (investment
vehicles), and without knowledge of construction (how to
integrate their investment program). Most don't even know
how much money they want to accumulate, and they think
nothing of getting their advice from in-laws. *As a matter of*

fact, most people don't even have a good idea of what money is. Considering the difficulty of the task of accumulating a fortune and the relative simplicity of building a house, doesn't it become obvious that failure in this case is far more likely than success?

This book is going to approach the problem in its entirety. It will familiarize you with the environment in which you'll be building your wealth (the economy); it will tell you how to plan your goals, what money and wealth really are, and will introduce you to some of the building materials (investments) that can get you where you want to go. When you finish, you'll be well on your way to becoming your own financial architect, and your chances of success at the single most difficult task in life will be increased a thousandfold.

IT STARTS WITH PRODUCTION—

Survival, comfort, happiness; these are the fundamental conscious and subconscious goals of all individuals. To achieve them, each person labors to produce some usable product that can either be consumed or traded with others for products that can be consumed. The farmer grows apples, some to eat now and some to trade with the tailor for clothes. With good fortune, he'll have a few left over at the end of each year, and these he'll try to store for consumption at a time when he no longer wishes, or is able, to produce. It's this storing away of unused production year after year, usually in the form of money, that leads to independent wealth. Wealth is nothing more or less than an accumulation of production (or claims on production); when an individual has accumulated enough wealth to supply his total consumption needs for as long as he may live, then he has achieved financial independence.

There are two steps that must be climbed; first, producing enough so that you have surplus production (wealth) left over at the end of the year; and second, and by far the most difficult, preserving and hopefully increasing that wealth by using it to acquire more of the same. The challenge lies in doing this year after year in an economy in which almost all the forces involved are directed toward thwarting your efforts and robbing you of all you've gained.

Your formal education, assuming you're a professional, has taken fifteen to twenty years, and this does not count the years of practical experience necessary to achieve high earning levels. These years of sacrifice have been aimed at one objective: to enable you to *earn*. Consider how much time and energy you've devoted to learning how to utilize your surplus earnings. Probably very little. If you're typical, you don't have a clear idea of what money is, let alone an understanding of the complex problem of the accumulation and preservation of great amounts of it. If you don't take time to learn what wealth is all about, you may find all the effort spent in developing a high earning ability has been wasted.

The objective of this book is to give you the expertise necessary to accumulate independent wealth using only your surplus production. To do this, you must understand enough about economics to be able to predict the future course of the economy by observing current events. In addition, you must recognize the relationships and relative values of all types of investment and savings vehicles, develop rational financial goals, and thereby design a strategy by which you can reach your goals in spite of external forces.

COMMONSENSE ECONOMICS—

Of all the subjects taught in high schools and colleges, none is as dry, as dull or as consummately boring as economics. Few people come away from their school years with anything but a distaste for this whole area of thought. It is obtuse, complicated and seems to have precious little bearing on the world in which they live. This view of economics is fundamentally false. Economics is, from the standpoint of both society and the individual, the one subject

that most influences the human condition. From cradle to
grave human beings must trade with others in order to survive,
and economics is the science of trade. To the extent that
natural economic laws are understood by the individual he
will prosper; to the extent they are understood and followed
by a society, that society will prosper. When civilizations rise
it is invariably true that they are, even if unconsciously,
following natural economic laws; and when they decline and
fall it is because they pervert or ignore these laws.

In the world of science, we marvel at the beautiful
simplicity that exists in nature; the endless interrelationships
of matter that follow smoothly functioning natural laws. As
scientists delve deeper and deeper into areas of the physical
universe, the patterns and systems become more and more
understandable. But in economics, the reverse seems true.
The more books that are written, the more incomprehensible
and complicated seem to be the patterns. It reminds one of
the evolution of witch doctors' potions which start as natural
remedies and after generations of mumbo-jumbo become
wild, senseless gyrations that are both useless and dangerous.

In practice, it seems that most economists reject the
scientific method as a valid approach to economics. They
don't appear to have firm starting points (postulates) for
their theories, and they fail to accept the fact that observation of past events is a useful tool. Consequently, history
repeats itself endlessly, one society following another into
economic oblivion, with the catastrophes of inflation, recession, depression and monetary loss never ending.

The truth is that there *are* starting points in economics.
There are laws of nature that apply to human beings and to
the interaction between humans in trade, commerce and all
money matters. Understanding some of these laws will open
your eyes to the true causes of the economic turmoil that
surrounds us and enable you, as it enables the physicist, to
predict the future.

In the last few years, the average American has had a

myriad of economic terms thrust upon him. Inflation, recession and devaluation have become household words and worries. Newspapers and magazines are filled with stories, articles and editorials about the economy. Yet, believe it or not, not one American in a thousand understands what is happening. There are authors that for years have tried to bring an understanding of real economics to the individual. The maverick economists (if you use the word "maverick" to denote a critter that doesn't go along with the herd), including Ludwig von Mises, Murray Rothbard and Henry Hazlitt, have written scores of books which have proven and reproven that current solutions to economic problems are nothing but the wildest idiot's folly. The problem is not that no one understands; it's that the solutions to man's problems which are offered by these laissez-faire economists are not acceptable to the interests that wish to politically control the lives and wealth of the world. It seems inconceivable that anyone, even those prestigious leaders of economic policy such as professors Paul McCracken and John Kenneth Galbraith, could read Henry Hazlitt's book, *Economics in One Lesson*,[1] and not understand the fallacies of their own programs.

You may have said that economics is too difficult for you to understand; you're more interested in your own situation and how to improve it. I take exception to that view. Economics is *not* hard to understand. It is, in reality, the simplest of all the sciences. When you get through with this chapter, you should have a sound knowledge about the way things *really* work and that knowledge is going to be your armor, your only armor, against the events that are going to financially devastate most individuals.

ECONOMICS IN ACTION—A MICROCOSM—

It is one of the wonders of science that no matter how small or insignificant a piece of matter is, it still obeys all the laws of nature that govern the largest masses in the universe.

Thus, a piece of stone no bigger than a pea will act and react according to the same mathematical formulas that govern a galaxy. The beauty is that a scientist can study the pebble and project his observations into an understanding of a galaxy. When Galileo dropped a small and a large object from the leaning tower of Pisa and determined that they both hit the ground at the same time, the recognition of the significance of this observation changed the course of science for all time.

It's my contention that we, too, can use this technique to gain an understanding of economic events. Further, I contend that in economics, as well as physics, the things that hold true on a small scale will be just as valid when applied to a large scale. We'll start by observing a small society, so small that it only consists of three families. The things you'll learn in this small society will enable you to understand equally well the forces at work within your worldwide society of three billion people. At least that's my contention. Judge for yourself.

In a small community, surrounded by mountains and completely isolated from the outside world, live three families: the farmers, the tailors and the carpenters. These three families toil all day long—six days a week, 52 weeks a year—and each produces a product. As you may have guessed, the farmers produce food. They have an orchard, a field and some animals, and they produce enough to supply themselves and to trade with the other families for their production. The tailors produce clothes and fabrics; the carpenters produce lumber and such useful items as tables, chairs and fences. Each family is skilled only in the production of its own goods; each has specialized and learned to trade its production for the products of others. For the sake of this discussion, let's measure their production in "units." In an average year, each family produces three units of production, and to live comfortably, each family consumes three units of production. A diagram of the production of the community is shown in Figure 1.

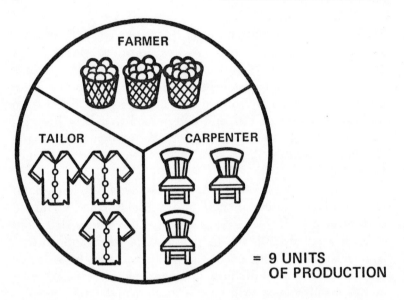

Figure 1

We can conclude that the total production of the community is nine units; its consumption is nine units; and therefore, its standard of living is nine units. Standard of living for our purposes will be defined as the total units of production which are consumed during a given time period by an entity, be it a whole society or an individual.

There are two possibilities for change in the standard of living of our community. First, the production of the community could rise. Second, the production of the community could decline. What could cause it to rise?

    1. The inhabitants work harder.

    2. They develop better production techniques.

What could cause it to decline?

    1. They could work less.

    2. They could forget how to produce efficiently.

    3. They could lose production from natural causes.

    4. They could lose production from vandalism or war.

Let's look at an increase in production first. If the farmer is successful in developing new planting techniques and produces twice as large a crop, our picture will look like this:

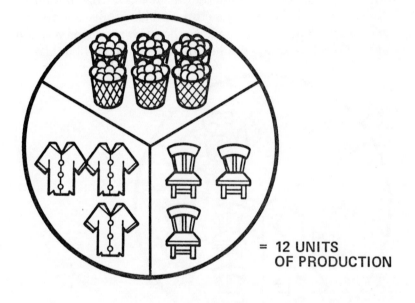

= 12 UNITS
OF PRODUCTION

Figure 2

Immediately, you recognize that the total production of the community has risen to 12 units. If they consume all the units, the standard of living of the community will have risen to 12. In other words, they are better off; they are more comfortable and better fed than they were before. If you also assume that a higher standard of living is something that is desirable, you would have to agree that things have improved.

Question: (Think carefully about this before you read further.) Assuming they consume the goods, *is there any way in which you could increase the production and not improve the standard of living of the community?* Since we've defined standard of living as the total goods consumed, it must be presumed that if the goods increase and the number of consumers does not, the standard of living must increase.

Now, take a second and even more revealing situation. What happens when production decreases? What if vandals destroy part of the farmer's crop, and his production for the year is only one-half as large? He has now produced one and one half units, and our production diagram looks like this:

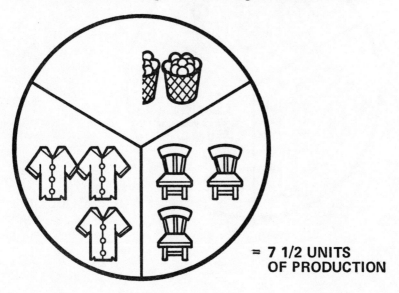

= 7 1/2 UNITS
OF PRODUCTION

Figure 3

The total production of the community has dropped to 7½ units, and the standard of living has decreased correspondingly. Each family now has a standard of living of 2½ units rather than three. They are worse off, right? Absolutely.

Now, here's question number two. Pay close attention. If you know the answer, which you probably will, you've taken a giant step toward being able to predict the future of the economy of the United States and the world. Inherent in this question and answer is the solution to every major economic problem facing the nation.

Question 2. If production *decreases,* can the standard of living increase? Can it remain the same? Or must it decrease? Remember, we are assuming a constant population that consumes all it produces. Look at Figure 3 and think. *You should be saying that obviously the standard of living must decrease if production decreases.* Obviously. If you are good at extrapolating and start with Question 2 and its solutions, you should now be able to answer the following question.

Which of the following programs are beneficial to a society, and which are destructive on an absolute basis?

1. Farm subsidy programs.
2. Wage controls.
3. Price controls.
4. Minimum wage laws.
5. Export tariffs.
6. Import tariffs.
7. Product boycotts (i.e., meat boycotts).
8. Anti-trust laws.
9. Grain acreage control programs.
10. Price control through destruction of livestock or other products.
11. Defense spending.
12. War.

If you can't apply these techniques to our small isolated society and thus arrive at an absolute answer, I'll give you a hand later on. Right now, I think you need some more background material on fundamental concepts. Let's talk about prices, money, banking and inflation.

PRICES

What is meant by price? In our little community, we might say that price is a ratio at which one commodity can be exchanged for another. For example, one unit of food is *priced at* one unit of construction. One unit of construction can then be traded for one unit of the tailor's work. It would look like this as an equation:

Figure 4

In the situation in which the farmer only produces one-half a crop, some price ratios will change if he exchanges one-third of his production for one-third of the production of the carpenter. Since he has produced only one and one-half units, he now exchanges one-half unit of his production for one whole unit from the carpenter. Thus, one-half unit of A equals one unit of B or C, and you might say that the price of farm goods has risen. The carpenter must pay the same amount for only one-half as much. Prices of farm goods have doubled in relation to other commodities. We have seen an *absolute* decline in the total production of the community. Goods are more scarce. There are only 7½ units where there were normally nine units.

But have we seen a *general* rise in prices? Farm goods have doubled, but what of other commodities? Hasn't the price of the carpenter's goods dropped? If price is a relationship, a ratio, we can certainly say that in relation to farm goods, the carpenter's products have dropped to half their former value. One-half a unit of the farmer's goods will now buy one whole unit of the carpenter's production. Thus, where one product has gone up in "price," the others have gone down.

You should be coming to a very interesting conclusion. In a barter society, there can be *no change in the general price level.* There can be no such thing as inflation! It can't be caused by scarcity, abundance, or even unions. One product can change in value in relation to the others; for example, if apples remained scarce, they would demand a higher price in terms of other goods. But those other goods would go down in relation to apples, and the general price level would not have changed. The other products, if their quantity remained constant, would not necessarily change in relation to each other. This isn't to say that the standard of living of the society won't change. Since it is based on absolute quantities of consumable products, when the amount of production goes up, the standard of living goes up; and when the amount of production goes down, the standard of living goes down. But prices? They are only relative ratios and remain constant.

Okay, then how do we have inflation? Simple. It is nothing more than an increase in quantity of the commodity used as the medium of exchange, while all the other commodities remain relatively constant. When the quantity of one commodity such as apples is increased, we know that they will become less valuable in relation to other commodities. It will take more and more of them to trade for the same number of some other product. If they grew as abundantly as leaves on every tree and anyone could have them for the picking, people certainly wouldn't be willing to trade their hard-worked-for products to obtain them. Any commodity that becomes abundant loses its value relative to the commodities that are useful but harder to produce. Thus, even gold, if it were as abundant as dirt, would be almost valueless as a commodity. It may have many uses, as does rock, but people would pay very little for it, because if it became too expensive they could dig their own.

Inflation, or as we normally use the word, a general rise in prices, is caused simply by an increase of the commodity known as "money." As "money" becomes abundant in relation to other commodities, the price of those commodities goes up relative to money. However, they may not go up in "price" relative to each other. One loaf of bread may still be exchangeable for one pound of apples, but both may jump from 10 cents to 50 cents as the amount of "money" in the society is increased.

MONEY

Before we go further, you're going to have to understand what I mean by money. If you've read Harry Browne's book *How to Profit from the Coming Devaluation*[2] (and I recommend it), you've already had a pretty good explanation of how money comes into being. It evolves from barter practices in almost every society. In our little three-family community, we could see it come into use. Assume the carpenter wants to buy a shirt from the tailor. If the tailor needs no carpentry work done, or if the value of the shirt is too low in relation to the table the tailor needs, the carpenter might use some other commodity he has on hand to trade—for example, some apples that he had left over from a trade with the farmer. In a barter society, any commodity that is desired by everyone in the community and can be divided into small trading units might easily become used as money.

The dictionary has several definitions for money, but most of them revolve around the idea that it is a commodity used as a medium of exchange. If the carpenter acquires apples from the farmer with the sole intention of using them as a medium of exchange, they most certainly have become money, and it should be easy to see that they could become a

fairly standard form of money in the limited community I
have described. Things could be priced in terms of apples,
and for smaller purchases, each family could keep a few on
hand just for trading.

In primitive societies, all manner of commodities have
been used as a medium of exchange. Cattle, for example, are
common as both a medium of exchange and a measure of
wealth in agricultural societies. On some Pacific islands, stones
have been used. North American Indians used beads or
"wampum." Not all of these things are practical as money, of
course. A medium of exchange that is to be most useful over
a long period of time should have certain characteristics.

First, if I'm going to take a commodity in on trade with
the hope of exchanging it with someone else for their
products, I should be sure it's something they'll recognize
and need. Then, I'll want to make sure it will last until I'm
ready to trade. Milk, for example, might spoil if I kept it
around too long and, therefore, would make a poor money.
It should be divisible so that I can make small purchases with
it, and there shouldn't be too much fluctuation in the
quantity available, as we've already determined that the value
of a product goes down as the quantity available goes up.
Further, it would help if the commodity was relatively rare,
so that a small amount was valuable. Then, a large purchase
wouldn't be impractical, and the accumulation of wealth
wouldn't present storage problems.

Money should take a certain amount of human energy to
create. If apples are to be successful as money, they must
represent the labor of the picker, grower, packer, etc. They
must also represent the labor that went into the capital
equipment necessary to aid the farmer in producing them, as
well as the creative ideas that were needed to make their
production easier. The value to you of any product depends
on your willingness to give of your production in order to
obtain it. That is, in a way, a measure of the amount of labor
it would take you to reproduce the item for which you're

trading. That value is made of human energy, ideas and the capital mechanism necessary to produce it.

Real money, as I see it, is a kind of condensed form of human energy and ideas. The apple produced by the farmer is an example of this. So is a gold coin. It represents the ideas, labor and equipment of the prospector, the miner, the smelter and the mint—all condensed into one small coin. Of course, the effort by itself is not enough to make a good money. It must also be a commodity that has other attributes: it is wanted, useful (even if only for its beauty), durable and divisible. Over the centuries and around the world, gold and silver have seemed to best fill the demand for a good money. They have all the attributes that make them nearly ideal: rarity, utility, divisibility, durability, and because of these attributes, they are universally recognized and desired.

INFLATION

We started by asking where inflation comes from, and now perhaps we're ready to see how it could come about. Suppose we look at a society that used gold as a medium of exchange. The ruler of a country has taken on the task of creating coins out of the gold with his image stamped on them. Let's imagine that this society has produced one hundred gold coins, and they are used to trade for one hundred units of other production. Thus, they have a value of one unit of production, and the units of production of the society would be said to cost one gold coin.

The ruler himself is involved in trading with these coins. Finding that he is unable to live on the amount he's able to tax from the people, he thinks of a scheme. Every time one of the coins passes through his hands, he files off a little of the gold from the coin. Let's assume that he files off five percent. When he trades each coin again for a unit of production, the person receiving it doesn't realize that he's really receiving less gold than he expected for his product. He

has come to believe that the coin represents a given weight of
gold. Gradually, all the coins in the realm pass through the
ruler's hands, and he now has enough gold filings accumulated to mint five new coins. He does this, and quickly spends
them. Now there is no more gold in circulation than there
was last year, but there are 105 coins in circulation and only
100 units of production.

1/100th of Total Gold Supply = One Unit of Production

1.05 Coins = One Unit of Production

Although it may not immediately become apparent, the
increased supply of coins (money) will soon be used to bid
for the available units of production (products), and the
relative value of each coin will fall. Rather than one unit of
production costing one coin, it will soon cost 1.05 coins.
Inflation has set in. People will soon be talking about rising
prices. Inflation would stop right there if the ruler stopped
filing coins, but if each year he continued to file off five
percent of the gold in all the coins of the realm, then
inflation would continue at a rate of 5% a year. First, it
would cost one gold coin to buy a product, then two, then
three, etc. Donald J. Hoppe, in his book *How to Invest in
Gold Coins*[3] tells about early Rome:

> "The earliest money of the practical Romans was
> neither gold nor silver but an ingot of copper—the
> as—weighing one pound. At first the as was passed by
> weight, but later it was stamped with the seal of the
> state, broken into smaller pieces and passed by sight.
> By the fourth century B.C., the as had evolved into a
> heavy round stamped copper slug, the as grave. With
> so large a coin passing by sight, the temptation
> surreptitiously to debase it by reducing its weight
> proved irresistible to authorities. By the middle of the
> third century B.C., the weight of the as had dropped
> to four ounces. By the end of the First Punic War,

around 240 B.C., it had shrunk to a mere two ounces,
and by 70 B.C., it weighed no more than half an
ounce."

In early times, filing, clipping or rubbing the metal off the
coins was not the only way rulers robbed the people. They
also alloyed cheaper metals with gold, and even created the
first "sandwich" coins of copper plated with silver. In Rome
in 15 B.C., Emperor Augustus established the "Aureus" at
126 grains of gold. In 60 A.D., Nero devalued it to 110
grains; Trajan again reduced it in 105 A.D.; by 200 A.D.,
under Severus of Caracallas' rule, it was down to 60 grains,
and by 268 A.D., under the rule of Gallienus, the coin no
longer contained any gold but was merely copper with silver
plating.

The history of currency debasement is intertwined with
the history of nearly every nation in the world. I'll have
more to say about modern techniques of debasement, but
first I should take the time to explain the evolution from
hard currency to paper money. It was this advance in "money
technology" that really opened the floodgates of economic
destruction.

BANKING

After the invention of paper and the printing press, the use
of receipts in trade became commonplace. You can imagine
how the evolution of banking might have taken place. A
person who had accumulated any significant amount of gold
or silver often found it safer to store his wealth with a
reputable gold dealer. That dealer would charge a storage fee
but would provide the safe vault necessary to protect against
theft. The depositor would receive a paper receipt for his
gold which would say something similar to "This is to certify
that John Doe has deposited 100 ounces of fine gold at my
bank and can withdraw it on demand," and it would be signed
by the owner of the depository. Gradually, these depositories
became known as banks and the receipts became known as
bank notes and were payable to the bearer.

The bankers soon discovered that a tidy profit could be made by loaning out the gold that had been deposited. By waiving the fee to the depositor and even offering him a rate of interest if he would agree not to withdraw his gold for a given period (a year, for example), they could then loan the gold and charge a higher rate of interest to the borrower, pocketing the difference. No one was cheated, and everyone received what was bargained for. The original depositor knew that there was some risk because the banker could fail to repay him, but a banker of good reputation found no lack of people ready to deposit gold and reap the profits of interest.

If the process stopped here, there would be no inflationary effect. The depositor has the unit of gold. He can trade it for a unit of production or hold it. No new unit of money is being introduced into the economy, and thus, there will be no resultant rise in prices. If the depositor chooses to remove the gold from circulation and not spend it (by depositing it in the bank), the economy will actually notice an apparent decrease in the money supply, and commodities would become cheaper in relation to gold. If the banker lends out the gold and the borrower spends it, it is no different than if the original owner had spent it. It is real wealth and is not inflating the money supply. Only now the borrower has the unit of production that the gold purchased, rather than the depositor. The depositor just has a receipt.

One thing could alter the apparent money supply, however. Suppose the depositor decides that before his gold is due to be repaid to him by the banker, he would like to make a purchase. He could take his receipt for the gold to a manufacturer and say "Sell me that wagon. I don't have gold right now, but this receipt can be exchanged for gold on the due date, and you can collect your money then."

At this point, if the manufacturer accepts the receipt in exchange for the wagon, we have seen our first inflation of the money supply, for now both the gold *and the receipt for the gold* have been used as purchasing media. Two units of production have been consumed, but only one unit of gold was used to pay for them. The supply of real money (the gold in circulation) has been increased by one paper receipt. If you followed the receipt back to its source, it would become apparent that it was the debt or note of the fellow who borrowed from the bank that was now being used as money. In other words, the individual that borrowed the gold from the bank had indirectly created a note which was now circulating in the community.

This process is known as "monetizing" debt. If the notemaker died and the note was never repaid, the community has lost a unit of its production which he consumed but never replaced with his own production. Anyone involved in the transaction might be the one to suffer the actual loss. It could be the banker if he makes good the gold receipt out of his own funds, even though the borrower never repaid him the gold. If the banker can't do this, the wagon maker, who now owns the gold receipt, would lose, for he now has nothing of value in exchange for his wagon. If he goes back to the original depositor and forces him to give back his wagon, or replace the worthless receipt with gold, it would then be the depositor who loses because he has lost the gold he deposited and has nothing to show for it.

The simple thing to remember in this analogy is that substitute money can be created in the form of an I.O.U., and if people in the community are willing to accept this I.O.U. in exchange for units of their production, the "money" supply in the community will be increased and prices will rise. Prices will rise because there is now apparently more money in circulation than there are products. If the debtor that originally creates the I.O.U. produces a product and redeems his note, the money supply will drop, and prices will fall back to their natural level. *But if the debtor repudiates his debt, someone in the community will have lost the production they originally traded for that note.* I hope that you are beginning to see that an increased money supply caused by monetized debt can be the cause of inflation. I also hope I have made it clear that a debt not repaid is a real loss to the community.

Let's take the next important step in analyzing the effect that this banker might have on the economy and on price levels. Suppose that the banker is approached by another person seeking a loan. He has no more gold in his vault, but he trusts the person applying for the loan, is sure he would be repaid on time and decides to take a chance. Since receipts that he has issued for gold on deposit have become accepted in the community in the past as money substitutes, he thinks to himself, "Why not just loan this person a receipt which will promise that the holder can redeem it for gold should they desire?" The banker's experience has told him that he usually has gold in the vault that people are storing, and most people would rather hold the receipt than the gold; therefore, it is unlikely that both receipts would be presented at once. What he has done is to double the supply of money substitutes in circulation in the community, and yet there is no product to back them up. If there were originally 100 pieces of gold and 100 units of production available to be purchased, there are now 100 pieces of gold *plus* two paper gold depository receipts that are being *used* as gold. There are now 102 units of purchasing power trying to be traded for 100 units of production, and the result is that the price of each unit of real production will now become 1.02 units of money.

If the banker continues and issues five or ten receipts for each unit of gold he has had deposited with him, he will place the economy of the village in increasing jeopardy. At some point, two or more of the holders of the receipts may decide to claim the gold that they believe they have on deposit, which will result in the banker become bank "rupt." In reality, the banker is taking I.O.U.'s from various people in the community, guaranteeing them, and then circulating them in the community as notes that are ostensibly as good as gold since the banker has said that he will redeem them for gold on demand. If nothing goes wrong and his creditors repay him on time with real production (or gold), he can then redeem his "banknotes" with the gold. No one is the wiser, and he has profited handsomely from the interest he charged the creditors.

This has been the history of currency inflation the world over. Bankers increase their own lending power by creating banknotes and back those banknotes with the credit of the borrowers. Money substitutes are created out of paper and ink, then flow into the market place to bid up the price of goods. These notes don't represent existing production, but rather *future* production. They create a debt against the future and a very real distortion of the economy. Unfortunately the inflationary effects of monetizing debt in this manner cannot easily be traced back to the source. Consequently individuals and organizations that are in reality the victims of inflation suddenly seem to be the culprits in the game.

THE GREAT FRAMEUP

There is a great deal of fuzzy thinking about where the responsibility for inflation lies (and here I mean the general rise in prices of commodities and services). Let's examine some of the more commonly blamed "culprits."

UNIONS

Many blame the unions, saying the increase in prices is due to excessive wage demands. In our simple barter-system community, when there were only nine units of production, what would the effect have been if one of the producers had demanded a higher price for his product? What if the farmer said, "rather than trading you for a unit of your production (a year's supply of clothes), I will raise my 'price' and demand two units of your production for one unit of mine." Now, since the tailor can only produce three units of production, he must either accept the food from the farmer at the farmer's price and have nothing left to trade at the old price with the carpenter or have nothing left to wear himself, or he must refuse to trade and leave the farmer with all his food. The tailor may trade one year, out of necessity, but the next year he will either spend part of his time growing his own food supply, or someone else will come in to compete with the farmer, since he has become excessive in his demands.

Actually, when the farmer made increased and unreasonable demands for his product, the effect on the community's price level was the same as when part of the farmer's crop was destroyed; that is, the price of the farm products rose but the price of the goods they were being traded for decreased proportionately. There was no change in the *general* price level. The difference is that the standard of living of the community did not decrease in this instance because the farmer still had the balance of his crop and could consume it himself. His standard of living went up, while the tailor's went down. Other things being equal, free enterprise would tend to prevent this from happening as the farmer would immediately be driven out of business by competition if he tried to demand more than his product was worth in terms of human labor, capital and ideas.

In this analogy, the unfair demands of labor are represented by the farmer, and in a community that did not have a paper money supply, unfair labor demands would simply wind up leaving the laborers out of work as either they would be fired, or the company for whom they worked would be forced out of business by competition. In any case, even if they received their raise and the company was not forced out of business by competition, *they would not have affected the general price level,* for when their products increased in price, the other products would fall in price proportionately. The laborers would be in a better position and the people they traded with in a poorer one, but only when the supply of money changed in relation to other commodities could there be inflation.

In conclusion, the unions aren't the culprits. Each union may have the power to raise the price of the product in which it is involved. If consumers are willing to pay the higher prices, then they must forego purchasing other items with those dollars.

Each union can only affect its own products, not prices in general. The blame has to be cast in another direction.

EXCESS PROFITS OF BIG BUSINESS

Many people would like to blame unfair profit demands of big business as the cause of rising prices. The same analogy used regarding unions still holds true. The price of one product in relation to other products cannot cause inflation whether the manufacturer raises the price or his laborers' wage demands cause the price increase. If the oil companies decide to increase gasoline prices in order to increase profits, they force a choice on you, the consumer. You must decide, when allocating your money, whether you value gasoline more than other items like food, clothes, and entertainment. If you do, you'll pay the higher prices for gas and forego the other things. The manufacturers of those other things will be forced to lower prices to continue marketing their products. Product prices are relative to one another; as one falls, the other rises. Like a teeter-totter. Only when all products are priced in terms of money can there be a general price rise and then only when the supply of money increases. It should be noted that if the money is real money (that is, a hard, usable commodity), the fact that its supply increases is not detrimental to the community.

If apples were the medium of exchange and there were suddenly an abundance of them, no one would be hurt because when an individual traded his production for a greater number of apples, he would be able to consume them. The real standard of living of the community would be increased. But when notes begin to be circulated in the community as substitutes for money and make a demand on the real production of the community, then real damage can be done. If the notes are never paid off, the persons holding them lose. While they are outstanding and circulating as money, prices are higher than they should be.

It should be realized at this point that prices could come down in two ways. The creditor can replace the note with real production, thus increasing the supply of products in the market-place and simultaneously reducing the supply of money substitutes, or the note can be repudiated, become recognized as worthless, and be destroyed. No new product has come into the community, but the supply of money substitutes has been reduced and thus prices of commodities other than the money commodity will fall.

No, big business is not the culprit either.

DECREASED SUPPLY OF PRODUCTS

It is held that increasing the supply of products will lower the rate of inflation. Since, as we have already discussed, the level of prices in any society is a ratio between the available products and the quantity of money bidding for those products, then it stands to reason that increasing the supply of products will lower the price level, providing the supply of money is not increased proportionately. There is no doubt the tremendous increase in production due to technological innovation that has occurred in the last fifty years in this country has camouflaged a great deal of the inflation, just as has the export of billions of dollars for foreign goods. But to attempt to cure inflation by saying we must produce more is to be exhorted by the hold-up man to work longer hours so you can replace what he is stealing. It does not diminish one whit the reality of the loss. Although you may not miss the standard of living you might have had without the past inflation, nevertheless, you have suffered.

A lower supply of products is not the cause of inflation; the cause is on the other side of the ledger.

DEFICIT SPENDING

If neither increased wage demands of labor, excessive profit demands of businessmen nor a lower supply of products is the cause of inflation, then what about the old saw that government spending results in inflation? Government spending, in excess of the hard money raised by taxes, is achieved through government borrowing. If the government borrowed gold from individuals, thus taking the purchasing power away from them and giving it to the government, this would not be inflationary. Because the gold was there, represented the production of those who held it, and could have been spent by them. However, the government doesn't do it that way. It borrows from a bank. The bank does not have gold. It takes the note or I.O.U. from the government, puts its guarantee on it, and gives it back to the government to spend in the society in the form of a bank note.* This is called "monetizing" debt. Remember? Whether the creditor is the government or an individual, the process is exactly the same. If you look in your wallet, you'll probably find some of these notes. They're called Federal Reserve Notes and are nothing more than monetized debt, representing no real production.

---

*The actual process by which the Government inflates the money supply is that it "attempts to sell securities to the public at a fixed price. If the public is not willing to purchase all of these *new* securities, the central bank intervenes in the securities market and purchases already outstanding Government securities from the public. In the process, the central bank gains an asset, the Government securities, and creates a liability, the money paid to the private sector which finances the purchase of the newly issued Government securities."[5]

Government deficit spending is definitely a cause of inflation. But not the only cause. For the fact is that inflation is caused by monetizing any kind of debt, whether it's an individual or government one. If the bank loans you money and has no hard money deposit to back it up, it is monetizing your note. In effect, it is taking your I.O.U., putting its stamp of approval on it and giving it back to you to spend. It then charges you interest for doing so. Now, this small transaction with you is in no way as significant as the $25-billion per year the government might borrow. But adding up all the individual and business loans made during the year and subtracting all the loans paid off during the same period will give you some measure of the increase in the total money supply contributed from the private sector of the economy.

For a clear illustration of the relationship between the money supply and consumer prices in the United States refer to Figure 5. The money stock (M_1) represents demand deposits of banks and currency in circulation.

How does the banking system arrange to loan money that it doesn't have on deposit? Through what is known as fractional reserve banking. When you deposit $100 in the bank, the bank can use that $100 as reserves and lend out a total of $666 to other borrowers. Where does it get the other $566? It doesn't even need the cash, for it merely credits the checking accounts of the borrowers. The Federal Reserve Board of Governors has the power to decide on the reserve requirements of all the banks in this country, and simply by changing the reserve requirements, can alter the money supply. For a detailed discussion of this system, read *Money & Markets; A Monetarist View* by Beryl Sprinkel.[4]

Add up the monetized debt of the government (which will never be paid off, incidentally), the monetized debt of the individuals and businesses, and you will understand the real source of inflation.

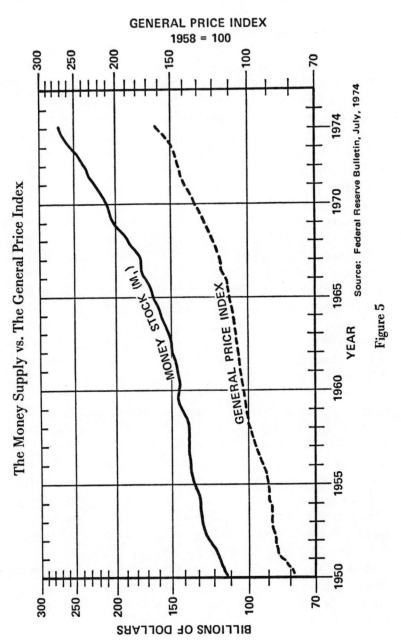

The Money Supply vs. The General Price Index

GENERAL PRICE INDEX
1958 = 100

MONEY STOCK (M₁)

GENERAL PRICE INDEX

YEAR

BILLIONS OF DOLLARS

Source: Federal Reserve Bulletin, July, 1974

Figure 5

> An inflation free society would be one in
> which no debt would be allowed unless the
> lender loaned only claims to hard commodi-
> ties. The elimination of monetized debt
> would eliminate inflation as we know it.

In all the discussions of inflation, rarely does anyone
mention the prestigious bankers of the world. Yet in the end,
who other than the banks really contributes to inflation?
Certainly they are co-partners with the government politicians who give them the monopoly to put the legend, "this
note is legal tender for all debts, public and private," on all
their notes. They must have the sanction of these politicians
and in return, they provide the money to elect them to
office. If you're interested in a history of the Federal Reserve
System, or some ideas on how the fractional reserve banking
system was started, I'd recommend *The Federal Reserve
System*[6] published by the Federal Reserve.

THE ESTABLISHMENT SMOKESCREEN

*"One difficulty about prescribing for inflation is that we
don't entirely know how serious the disease is. . . . . . The
argument made by those who demand very low rates has
simply been inconclusive."* (Paul McCracken, former Chair-
man of The Council of Economic Advisors.)[7]

Let's scrutinize the above statement. The history of
civilization is, in reality, the history of a series of societies, or
nations, as you might call them. The people in each nation
have come under the control of the leaders of a state or
government by force or by vote. In either case, the leaders of
the country (with the cooperation of the bankers) have
always and in every case found it necessary to increase their

funds beyond the amount they could collect through taxation. This is almost always done through some form of currency debasement. Whether the state borrowed from banks and monetized the debt, clipped coins or simply ran printing presses to print new issues of notes, the results have always been the same: rising prices. As the state monetized debt and consumed the products and services purchased with those I.O.U.'s, the community as a whole was deprived of that production. The fact that the community felt it was receiving tangible wealth back in the form of "money" only served to confuse it. In the end, the confusion that resulted from this illusory wealth caused a fatal cycle of events that ultimately ended in the collapse of each state involved.

If you as an individual borrow money from someone and never repay that person, you have stolen from him. You are a thief. He is worse off; he has lost some of his wealth. When a state monetizes debt either by printing bank notes directly or by borrowing such notes from a bank without intention of repaying, it is just as much a thief of the society. The difference is that the victim becomes twice removed from his enemy. He can't tell by whom he has been victimized. The real loss falls on the population as a whole, and in such a camouflaged pattern that the results defy surface analysis. In other words, the theft is translated into rising prices, and the rising prices do the dirty work. When the victim feels the threat and tries to protect himself, he usually flails out at the symptom rather than the cause. The theft occurs when a person borrows money and does not repay it. The symptom is the rising price. As the individuals in society attempt to react to the symptom (rising prices), the trouble begins.

When the Congress voted to increase the national debt, as they just did in June of 1974, how did you feel? Do you realize that what they're doing is borrowing money directly from *you* with no intention of ever paying it back? (Borrowing it from you, if you're a producer. Of course, if

you're on welfare or unemployed, you have nothing to lend
them.) Would you consider loaning someone money knowing
that they had a long history of debt repudiation, and
knowing that you may not agree with what they will do with
the money once they've borrowed it? Of course, you
wouldn't. But you're doing it anyway.

SYMPTOMS OF AN INFLATING MONEY SUPPLY—

The most staggering revelation to come from a study of
the economic history of past societies is that the sequence of
economic events in the United States during the past fifty
years has occurred repeatedly in dozens of other societies
stretching as far back as early Macedonia:

1. Government needs more money than it is able to
collect through taxation, so it issues paper money (or
clips coins);
2. When the government spends this new money,
business picks up;
3. As the increased supply of money percolates down
through the society, prices begin to rise and business
begins to slump;
4. To counteract the slump, the government issues
more money;
5. Business picks up again, prices begin to rise,
business slumps again;
6. People begin to distrust paper currency and begin
to hoard gold and silver coins;
7. Government points finger of blame at gold hoarders and passes laws to stop hoarding (often confiscat-
ing gold, sometimes silver);
8. More inflation: prices begin to rise more steeply,
people demand action and government passes price
and wage control laws;
9. Shortages appear: rationing begins, black markets
take over in place of regular markets;
10. Speculation begins to replace prudent investing

as capital markets fluctuate up and down due to the business cycles;

11. Hard work falls into disrepute; people get rich (or poor) speculating; the thrifty lose all to inflation; more and more people go on relief as production falls and inflation forces prices out of the reach of the elderly and marginal producers;

12. As more people go on relief, government must tax the remaining producers more heavily until they decide to stop producing, and the situation begins to compound itself;

13. Stock markets oscillate wildly up and down, and finally drop; marginal businesses fail; prices fall to natural levels; currency is devalued to real levels; debts are repudiated; the country begins again.

The above scenario has been repeated in almost every society where the state has debased the currency. Everyone who is concerned about preserving his wealth should read *Fiat Money Inflation In France* by Andrew Dickson White.[8] It is a classic chronicle of the effect that fiat money had on the economy of France subsequent to the French revolution. The parallels between France in 1789 and the U.S. in the 20th century are both obvious and frightening.

One has to wonder if President Roosevelt had ever studied the histories of countries that tried outlawing gold and inflating the money supply to solve their temporary economic problems. When he said, "it's all right; after all, we're borrowing from ourselves," had he heard of Macedonia, or the French economy of 1789? And what of President Nixon? When he instituted price controls, where were the scientists who said, "Let's observe the past before we act." If the saying is true that history repeats itself, could it be because no one consults history before they act? For Dr. McCracken to say that we don't really know the seriousness of the disease called inflation is totally absurd. The disease is *fatal*.

THE STATE SOLUTIONS TO INFLATION—
FIGHT THE SYMPTOMS—

As the U.S. nears election time the cries for programs to fight inflation rise among the political hopefuls. Every politician places the blame for our spiraling prices squarely on the lack of decisive action by present administration officials. In a sense, they are right; inflation could be stopped by cutting out the cause. But unfortunately, those would-be office holders, if elected, won't attack the real cause of inflation. If elected, they'll only make matters worse; for what they want to do is spend vast quantities of time and money fighting the *symptoms* of inflation. The political solutions to inflation are pretty well summed up by Paul McCracken in his *Fortune* interview previously cited. His cure for inflation revolves around the following elements:

1. Fiscal responsibility.
2. Federal job-training programs.
3. Stronger anti-trust laws.
4. Control over unions.
5. Sustain the present program of wage price controls.
6. Pass laws regarding prices calling excessive price increases "an abuse of economic power."

In light of our foregoing analysis of the causes of inflation, let's examine his "cures" one by one.

Fiscal responsibility by government is as attainable as a magic wand. Anyone who thinks the next administration will be elected to office based on the promise that they will scrap the elaborate something-for-nothing welfare schemes of the previous administrations, doesn't understand the problem. Government costs are rising and will continue to rise.

What of number two? Federal job training programs are considered necessary because of the vast armies of unemployable, uneducated workers. Why are they unemployed? Because they have no skills. But to tell you the truth, no one is born with a skill. Every human being has had to learn one

in order to become a producer, and assuming we've never had
to rely on the government to tax us for the money to train
these people before, why now? Because the system has made
these people unemployable. The very minimum-wage laws
that were effected to raise their standard of living have thrown
them out of work. (See page 40 on Minimum Wage Laws.)
They are not worth $2.00 an hour, and taxing the people to
pay for training to make them worth $2.00 an hour is not the
answer. The answer lies in letting the market be free to pay
them what they are worth, and if individually they want
more than that, they are free to educate themselves. But to
insinuate that the unemployment of these people is in any
way a cause of inflation is a rank absurdity.

Stronger anti-trust laws? In theory anti-trust laws were en-
acted to foster competition by preventing large companies
from forcing smaller firms out of business. Granted, no company should be allowed to use *coercion* to damage another
company, but analysed properly, it lowers everyone's standard of living to prevent businesses from properly utilizing
their capital and know-how to produce their products in the
cheapest possible ways. In effect anti-trust laws say that
even if it's cheaper for two companies to sell their product
if they join together versus operating as separate companies,
no matter, they can't do it. The businesses that can't compete with the lower prices of the more efficient comglomerate
scream that they should be subsidized, and that competition
is unfair if it undersells them.

Nonsense. The consumer gets the best deal when the
product is cheapest, and the product is cheapest when people
can freely compete in the marketplace. The only monopolies
that work to the disadvantage of the individual are those
that are created and protected by the bureaucracy itself.
As an example to prove the point, the U.S. Post Office would
be out of business in six months if small businessmen were
allowed to compete in the delivery of first-class mail.

Even if monopolies could fix prices at a level above what

they should be, it wouldn't cause inflation. It would simply reallocate the resources of the individual consumer, as occurred in the example of excessive demands of big business and unions.

Control over unions? We have already discussed the fact that unions can have no lasting effect on prices if there is no government interference. They do not increase the money supply, and since an increase in the money supply is the *only* thing that can lower the value of money, unions are not guilty. They may cause the price of automobiles to rise. They may even cause a few companies to collapse. But they do *not contribute one iota* to the general rise in prices known as inflation.

Sustain the present program of wage-price controls? Suppose that the farmer in our little community is told that he cannot sell one unit of his apples for one unit of the carpenter's work. He must charge less. His price is now controlled and he must sell 2 units for 1. Immediately, his standard of living must go down, for he will trade off one unit of apples and only get one-half unit in return. He has two choices: he can trade, or he can refuse to trade. If he trades, he is less well off, and if this continues, he will probably go into another line of work where he can attain better rewards for his labor. If he doesn't trade, at least he still has his apples; but now a shortage of apples appears on the market, and the others must do without. Their standard of living drops or, at least, is distorted.

Since rising prices are nothing more than a symptom of an increasing supply of the money commodity, trying to hold them down will have about as much success as putting Bandaids on measles. The fact is that not only will price controls be useless against inflation, they will have the effect of forcing producers to suspend production by making production unprofitable. This will lead to shortages. When the shortages appear, the government will say it must handle the allocation of the few supplies available, and we then have rationing. Rationing always leads to black markets. Remember World War II? If this is not readily apparent to you, read the headlines of every paper for most of 1973. Gas shortages, fuel shortages, meat shortages, grain shortages, paper shortages. And everywhere products available at twice the price on the black market. Did you think this was just coincidental? Or did you make the connections between the price controls and the shortages?

The final and saddest of all the responses to this money-supply inflation is that in the end, the propaganda mechanism of the government points the finger at the very businessmen who are being damaged the most by the system. Without fail, the public, outraged and frustrated by its inability to cope with inflation, assumes that it must be the producer himself that is the cause. Now, you have the worst injustice of all, the product boycott. Housewives marching outside the butcher shop, picketing the merchant, and in the end driving him out of business. With him, go the meat-packers and with them go the cattle farmers. As we already know, when you destroy production, down goes the society's standard of living.

The great Austrian economist, Ludwig von Mises summed up the establishment's response to the failures of these wage and price control programs:

> "History is a long record of price ceilings and anti-usury laws. Again and again emporers, kings, and revolutionary dictators have tried to meddle with the market phenomena. Severe punishment was inflicted on refractory dealers and farmers. Many people fell victim to persecutions which met with the enthusiastic approval of the masses. Nonetheless, all these endeavors failed. The explanation which the writings of the lawyers, theologians and philosophers provided for failure was in full agreement with the ideas held by the rulers and the masses; man, they said, is intrinsically selfish and sinful, and the authorities were unfortunately too lax in enforcing the law. What was needed was more firmness on the part of those in power."[9]

Will the new Ford administration, currently disavowing the use of wage and price controls, really have an effect on inflation? *Time Magazine*[10] in its September 9, 1974 issue puts to rest the idea that things will improve. It says that Walter Heller, one of Ford's advisors,

> "will propose a wide-ranging program featuring a Government wage-price agency that could subpoena company and union records, order large increases suspended... and even roll back 'really flagrant' boosts. Other Heller ideas that are widely backed by liberals include: easing in Federal Reserve monetary policy to head off a recession; credit controls to channel more loan money to home builders and buyers...; a huge Government program to hire the unemployed for public service jobs; tax cuts of $6 billion to $8 billion..."

These cosmetic approaches to inflation are almost without exception inflationary in themselves: creating paper money to pay the unemployed; cutting taxes so the Government must meet its budget by printing more fiat money; easing the Federal Reserve monetary policy. The article goes on to state

> "Federal Reserve Chairman Arthur Burns and Presidential Counsellor Kenneth Rush favor more Administration 'jawboning' against big wage and price boosts. President Ford himself asked for and signed into law last week a bill creating a new Council on Wage and Price Stability...."

Inflation is not caused by rising prices. Rising prices are a result of inflation. All the price controls, whether through jawboning or at the point of a gun, are exercises in futility.

To assume that any party would, or could, have any long term answers to the country's economic problems is folly. To plan your own financial future based on the belief that this administration or the next, or the next, will provide us with the leadership and programs that will finally cure inflation will most certainly lead to your financial demise.

THE MYTH OF
GOVERNMENT ECONOMIC PROGRAMS—

Before leaving the subject of government "solutions" to our economic woes, I think I should take time to cover some other political fiascoes.

Earlier in the book, I said that when you apply any set of conditions to a simple three-family society, you should be able to arrive at the same results as though you applied the conditions to a society of three billion. Also, I mentioned that there was a simple way to tell if a government program was beneficial or detrimental in the long run. If you remember, I asked the question: "Is there any way you can decrease production in a society and simultaneously increase the standard of living?" For example, could a lone hermit spend half as much time gathering food as he has in the past and be better off? It seems fairly obvious that the answer is *no*. Here's the magic question that you should ask yourself when someone suggests a "program" for improving the country. In the long run, *does the application of the program tend to increase or decrease production?*

AGRICULTURAL CONTROLS

Let's take some of the government programs, one at a time. In the thirties and late forties, farmers lobbied to maintain price levels in the face of falling farm prices, claiming they were being forced out of business due to the low prices. In response, Congress passed a number of agricultural acts extending back into the thirties. The purpose of these acts was to protect the farmer: the result was land taken out of production by paying the farmer not to grow crops, meat production reduced by having livestock slaughtered and buried, and foodstuffs made scarce by the purchase and destruction of enormous quantities of other farm products. The incredible stupidity of the process was told in a story in *Life* magazine in the March 20, 1950 issue. They tell of how the government spent $500 million on potatoes to support the price, but then couldn't figure out what to do with them:

> "The Agriculture Department then sprayed blue dye on its sacks of potatoes, to keep them from being sold for human consumption, and dumped them back to farmers for use as animal feed and fertilizer. But the dye colored only the top potatoes in the sack, and there grew a strong suspicion that many farmers simply threw away the colored ones and sold the others right back to the government, thus cashing in a second time. Finally the government offered to sell its surplus to needy foreign countries at 1 cent per 100-pound sack, one of the greatest bargains ever recorded. Unfortunately potatoes are so difficult and expensive to ship that even at this remarkable price there was trouble finding takers; the best customer was a man from Spain who said he could use 50,000 tons, chiefly because the sacks in which they were packed would be worth around 30 cents each in his country. There things stood until last month, when the government's stocks had mounted to 50 million tons and everybody was getting desperate. Then the Agriculture Department found a new method to dye the potatoes with a colored salt that is supposed to seep down into the sack and touch every single one. It now appears that the potatoes will all be used for hog feed or dumped into fields to rot into fertilizer. Potatoes aren't really much good as fertilizer, but even so this is probably the best possible solution because the potatoes were bound to rot anyway, and an outlying field is the ideal place."[11]

Potatoes weren't the only problem commodity, the article goes on to say:

> "In addition to the 76 million pounds of dried eggs which will never be eaten and the potatoes which will rot, the government has accumulated a vast amount of other stuff. Most of it, fortunately, is more edible or useful than the dried eggs and less prone to spoilage than the potato; in fact it is perfectly good farm produce and would be very

useful to have if only someone could figure out what
to do with it. To put the size of the surpluses into
everyday terms, the government has enough:

WHEAT to bake 12 loaves of bread for every man,
woman and child in the world.

CORN to make all the cornstarch, corn sugar, corn
syrup and corn oil that the U.S. will use in the
next five years.

BUTTER to bake a birthday cake for every child
under 15 in the U.S. for the next 10 years.

COTTON to produce 54 house dresses for every
U.S. woman.

PRUNES to give every member of Congress a dish
for breakfast until approximately September of
the year 3239."

In light of the foregoing discussion and assuming that you
agree that you can't enjoy a higher standard of living if you
have less to eat, were these agricultural acts beneficial or
detrimental to the country?

MINIMUM WAGE LAWS

In 1938, the government passed the Fair Labor Standards
Act which included the first minimum wage law. They said
no one, with the exception of agricultural workers, domestic
help, and retail trades workers, could be paid less than 25
cents per hour. The minimum wage was then raised to 49
cents in 1939, 75 cents in 1950 and so on until it reached
$2.00 in 1973. Was this good or bad? If it is good for the
country if production increases and bad if it decreases, let's
apply the situation to our small community and see the
direct effect.

Suppose the state says the farmer cannot pay his apple
pickers less than one bushel of apples per week. If these
workers don't pick enough to justify that wage, the farmer
might begin to lose money at his business. He would soon lay
off those workers and stop producing apples. Losing this
production would be detrimental to the standard of living of
the community, and the workers would be affected most

because they would be unemployed. Granted that if they were efficient workers and there was ample profit in the employer's product, he might be able to raise their wages and still produce. In fact, he might be able to raise the price of apples to compensate for the increased labor costs. But it would still be taking production away from the carpenter or tailor and lowering their standard of living if he raised his price.

In reality, a minimum-wage law has the absolute effect of driving the marginally-profitable producer out of business and leaving all the unskilled laborers unemployed. The very law that is designed to aid the poorest workers only succeeds in throwing them out of work and cutting the supply of products available to the community. Everyone loses. No wonder Dr. McCracken calls for federal job training programs for the unemployed. It seems only fitting that the bureaucracy that causes a worker to lose his job should retrain him for another. Pity that you and I and the apple farmer have to pay for that retraining through taxes.

EXPORT CONTROLS

On a number of occasions in the past, Congress has passed laws controlling exports. In 1973, bills were introduced to limit the export of cotton, wheat and various other commodities. The reason suggested was that we couldn't afford to lose these products which were in such short supply. Does this tend to increase or decrease production?

It must be assumed that a producer will try to sell his product to the highest bidder and also that a larger demand for a product will result in more of that product being produced. Generally, a greater demand, although initially causing a higher price, eventually results in lower cost, as production facilities are improved to supply the increased demand.

Establishing export controls decreases the size of a producer's market. Secondly, it prevents him from obtaining the maximum price for his production, as the only reason a person would ship his products out of the country rather than sell them locally is that the foreigners are willing to pay more. If other producers can export and he cannot, those exportable products will be more profitable. It will tend to limit the production of one item in favor of another. To say that the production is lost to the community when it is exported is nonsense; if the farmer trades with the carpenter, it doesn't matter whether the carpenter is in his valley or in another state or another country. He still has the benefit of the carpenter's work when he makes the trade. If the U.S. ships wheat to Japan and in return Japan ships automobiles to the U.S., the rise in wheat prices due to lower wheat supplies here is offset by the decrease in auto prices due to increased auto supplies.

TARIFFS

If I have $20.00 and an inefficient apple farmer offers me apples at $5.00 a bushel, I'll be able to buy four bushels. If he produced apples efficiently, I might be able to buy them for $4.00 a bushel and would then be able to buy five bushels. My standard of living would have increased by one bushel.

In a natural society, competition tends to increase everyone's standard of living by forcing producers to maximum efficiency. As soon as an artificial monopoly (i.e., one established and enforced by state edict) is granted a producer, he no longer has to work as efficiently; consequently, either his product quality drops, his production goes down or both. When this happens, the value of his product in relation to others in the marketplace changes. The price goes up.

A tariff is imposed because the cost of goods from another country is lower than the cost of goods locally and the local producers want to be protected from competition. The government, in order to protect the local producer, charges a tariff, or a tax, on the incoming goods. This keeps the local apple producer in business, for he is now able to get $5.00 per bushel. The person buying the apples is less well off because now he only has four bushels, where, had he been allowed to buy the lowest priced commodity, he would have had five. There is less production available to be consumed in the community, and the standard of living is lower. In effect, the government has protected the poor producer at the expense of the society.

"Yes," someone once asked me, "but what would happen if Japan were to produce an automobile essentially equivalent to the Ford, and were able to sell it here for one-half the price of the Ford. What would happen to all the workers employed at Ford?" It's simple; they would lose their jobs unless they were able to produce the Ford at competitive prices. What damage would be done? Well, there would be a lot of people on the labor market who would have to find a way of earning a living that provided a better or cheaper product to the market at competitive rates. To say that these inefficient producers should be subsidized at the expense of the community as a whole is absurd no matter how large a labor force they represent. They merely drag down everyone else's standard of living. It would be an extension of this haywire philosophy to say that if I invented a magic wand that could produce automobiles out of thin air, the magic wand should be destroyed for the benefit of the community, as it would throw the automobile workers out of a job. (With that kind of philosophy, the Garden of Eden would be a place to be shunned because everyone there is out of work.) Furthermore, by that logic, it would benefit the community to destroy the efficient mechanisms that have already been invented for rapid production, for if you once say you must not produce efficiently for fear of throwing people out of work, then where do you stop? Every person who stops producing one product is freed to produce some other item that is useful. When all the automobile workers are thrown out by my magic wand, they can start building swimming pools, and everyone who formerly had only a car can now have both a car and a swimming pool. Thus, the standard of living of the community will be raised.

Recently the rising wages of newspaper printers in New York drove many newspapers out of business. The Daily News, faced with a strike for higher wages, went to total automation to print its papers. The unions screamed. What's *your* opinion?

DEVALUATION—

One piece that we can hardly overlook in this economic puzzle is the cause and effect of devaluation. To understand it, let's go back to the banker who issues more receipts for gold than he has in his vault. When the time comes that people realize this and come forward to claim their gold (before it's all gone), the banker is faced with two alternatives. He can refuse to give them the gold at all, or he can offer to give them less gold per receipt than they had originally been promised. He also has the option of trying to collect the gold from all the people to whom he lent the receipts. (That is, he could demand payment of all outstanding notes, but assuming that those people had not yet produced a product but had merely consumed the loan, collection would be impossible.)

If the banker refuses to redeem the receipts, they would become worthless as they could represent nothing. If he redeems them for a partial value, they have been "de"-valued. In the United States in the 1920's there was a tremendous expansion of bank credit.* When the Federal Reserve began to constrict credit in 1929 the stock market collapsed and concomitantly people and businesses were unable to meet their loan commitments. The depositors of the banks tried to

---

*This expansion and subsequent contraction is chronicled and analysed in *America's Great Depression*, by Murray N. Rothbard (Los Angeles, Calif., Nash Publishing, 1972).

redeem their banknotes for gold, found there wasn't enough gold to meet redemptions and the panic began. The government under President Roosevelt realized that if everyone came in and claimed the gold that was rightfully his, there would be far more receipts turned in than there was gold available. This would quickly cause the banks involved (and they were all involved) to go bankrupt, along with the federal government. In addition, he wanted to embark on a program of spending in order to "stimulate" the economy.

To save the banking system and stimulate the economy, two things were necessary. First, the people could not drain the gold from the system and thus prove the bankruptcy to be true, and secondly, new "money" must be created without the public being able to redeem gold for their new money substitutes. The answer was exactly the same as that tried by the French legislature in the 1780's. He made it illegal to own gold and called in all the gold which was being held in private hands. This was an absolute fraud on those producers who had produced a product, exchanged it for gold and then taken a receipt for the gold. Now, they were told that in the "national interest" they could not have their gold back, nor could they own gold at all. In the future, they must be content to accept paper money as their sole measure of wealth. With this accomplished, the government had a free road toward printing all the money substitutes they might want.

Only one problem still presented itself. While the President could deny Americans the right to own gold, he couldn't extend that prohibition to foreigners. If trade was to continue between America and other countries, those countries would demand to be paid for their products in some form of currency that was convertible into gold. Therefore, he created a situation in which Americans couldn't redeem dollars for gold but foreign banks could. The obvious result was that while prices of American products and services began to rise, foreign goods did not. The foreign car and the foreign vacation became more and more a bargain. Why? Because when you bought a Volkswagen from Germany, the German manufacturer knew he could take that dollar and convert it into gold at any time. He was essentially being paid in gold, and gold being a commodity, there could be no inflation of that supply. As long as the U.S. was willing to redeem American Dollars in gold, the foreign producers were able to essentially avoid inflation when selling to American buyers. Those dollars that went overseas were replaced by products here in our economy. We rid our money supply of $2,000.00 and got a Volkswagen in return.

What did this mean to us? That we were able to maintain lower prices domestically. Because price is a function of the money supply versus the supply of all other commodities, when you increase the supply of commodities and decrease the supply of money (or money substitutes), the general prices are lower. By shipping billions of paper dollars abroad and bringing in exchange billions of usable, consumable products, we had a higher standard of living and lower prices. But anyone with a sense of real economics should have been able to predict the ultimate outcome. Soon the number of dollars abroad would build up beyond the supply of gold in the Treasury, just as earlier the supply of paper dollars in the U.S. had built up beyond the supply of gold. Then the government would be in exactly the same boat that it was in when the American people began to try to redeem their dollars for gold. There was a run on the gold supply and the government had to choose between continuing to redeem at its earlier agreed-upon price ($35.00 per troy ounce), and quickly running out of gold, thus admitting its bankruptcy, or redeeming for less than it had agreed upon, or refusing to redeem at all.

President Nixon happened to be at the helm when the final run on the treasury gold was imminent, and his solution was the same as that of President Roosevelt. Stop redemptions. He could not make it illegal for foreigners to own gold, but he could stop redeeming dollars, which he did.

Now, step back and think about this from the foreigner's point of view. They sold us a Volkswagen. They, in good faith, took back two thousand American dollars, with the understanding that they could convert this amount to gold at $35.00 per ounce. We were happy enough to have the Volkswagen at that price, and they were pleased to have the gold. Now we renig. We say "Sorry, old chums. We changed our minds. You can't have the gold." Where does that leave them? They entered into the contract in good faith, and by anyone's standards, they've been cheated. Well, immediately the price of the Volkswagen must jump to its true value in relation to other products, and the foreigners are stuck with buying products with those American dollars which no longer can be converted into gold. By now, the price of gold has begun to jump on the free market, since the U.S. has stopped selling at $35.00 per ounce. If they want gold, they must pay $75.00, $100.00, or $150.00 per ounce. Their other alternative is to buy commodities other than gold, an option they have previously refused since gold was a much better buy. Now, they must come back into the American economy and buy commodities at the prices Americans have had to pay. They have lost.

What about us? Well, Secretary of the Treasury, Schultz, said that the devaluation of the dollar and the suspension of gold sales really wouldn't affect the American worker too much. On the *Today Show,* just after the first devaluation, he indicated that perhaps French wines would go up in price, but other than that, we would be helped. For example, he indicated there would be a great surge in employment as foreigners became customers for American goods which would now be more attractively priced for them. That certainly sounded good. With California wines equal to French wines anyway, there wouldn't be much of a loss, and we could use those new jobs. What a boon to America, this devaluation!

But look again. Look at the real economics involved. What's happening now is that we're all paying for the years of low-priced products we've all enjoyed. We're about to make up for all that time that prices didn't rise as they should have because we were shipping dollars overseas and taking products back in their place. Now, those paper dollars will flow back into the economy, buying up products, bidding higher than you can bid for American production. They'll take the products out of the marketplace and replace them with paper money. And you know what happens: increase the money supply and simultaneously decrease the consumable goods, and you have a potentially disasterous rise in prices facing you. We will see higher rates of price increases in the future than we had ever dreamed possible. It's already happening.

Have you heard about the Japanese buying up real estate in California, or about the Arabs buying hotels in Florida, or about the "grain drain?" These things aren't coincidental; they aren't coming about as a matter of chance or because these foreigners are trying to destroy us. They want their money's worth for the products we bought from them. And they deserve their money's worth. I can't think of a more immoral stand than that suggested by some "economists" who say that we should pass laws to prevent them from buying our property. Nonsense. We took their products and gave them a claim check on our goods. Now it's time to honor our contract and let them buy whatever they want. It's bad enough that we refused them the original thing we promised (the gold). Let's not show ourselves to be totally immoral and not take the claim checks back at all!

Suppose you built a chair, went to the farmer and traded with him for six bushels of apples. But rather than taking them with you, you asked him if you could pick them up later. "Sure," he says, and gives you a claim check good for the six bushels. Later, you return with the claim check, and he says, "Sorry, I can't honor that claim check any more." Perhaps he offers you half as many apples, or perhaps no apples at all, but instead a dozen beets. Would you consider this man to be moral? More than likely, you'd either demand your chair back or insist that he honor his word; and you might even decide to get a gun to make him do it. In other words, this is the kind of immorality that leads to war.

GOLD

More and more over the last forty years, we have heard the politicians and spokesmen for politicians tell us that gold is outmoded as a medium of exchange. Lord Keynes called it a "barbaric metal." George Schultz said,

> "The rigidities of such a system [gold based] subject to the uncertainties of gold production, speculation and demand for industrial uses cannot meet the needs of today."[12]

We hear a lot of talk about international solutions to the currency problem; demonetizing of gold, use of Special Drawing Rights (SDR's), and some miracle that will be pulled off by the International Monetary Fund. What one must realize is that when you trade the product you produce for any "money" that is in itself a money substitute, if that money substitute is issued by an entity that can inflate the supply at whim, you are going to be worse off. Between the time you take that receipt for money and the time you trade it for something you want, its value will go down. The farther removed those receipts become from being related to physical production, the more likely it is that you will suffer a very real loss of purchasing power.

There is only one reason that the international bankers and governments want to sever the ties between currencies and gold, and it's not because gold would not handle the problems of trade. It is because they cannot inflate the supply of money if that money is tied to gold. And if they cannot inflate the supply of money, they cannot take the production from you that they would like without your knowledge. The concept that we don't need to tie money to gold (or any other real commodity) because the dollar is backed by the productive capacity of the nation sounds good but is pure nonsense. It's only realistic if you are able at any time in the future to take the money and exchange it for the same amount of production that you gave away when you took the money in trade originally. Unless the money is tied to a commodity such as gold, this will never happen.

Why Gold? There is nothing magical about gold.

When you see a bumper sticker that says STOP INFLA-TION, DEMAND GOLD, it is correct. If we used gold as the backing for all currency, there would be no inflation, but the same holds true if you say, STOP INFLATION, DEMAND POTATOES. It is the concept of backing the money substitutes with a real commodity, the supply of which can't be expanded at the whim of the politicians or bankers. Most commodities don't meet the requirements. Potatoes wouldn't keep. Furthermore, if they became the medium of exchange, the supply is too elastic and might increase drastically because everyone would start growing them and, therefore, their value would fall in relation to other commodities. Secondly, they are a real problem to store and transport, and they are far from uniform in quality. They would, however, be better than paper. Since we're looking for something that is recognizable by everyone, desired, divisible, durable and of relatively limited quantity, gold seems to fill the bill. Silver would too, as well as copper, platinum and diamonds, but as you think about it, gold might be the best.

"THERE AIN'T NO SUCH THING
AS A FREE LUNCH"—

Somewhere about 50 pages ago, we began to talk about economics and you; hopefully, the realization has come that there is no such thing as something for nothing. If a product is to be eaten, it first must be produced. Yet, throughout history the politicians have tried to prove the contrary and have been so eloquent in their arguments that they've lulled society after society into expecting miraculous abundance from sleight of hand—borrowing from ourselves, creating money when none exists, plundering the future. These are not answers to a more abundant life. It is unlikely, however, that politicians will ever change; nor is it the intent of this book to try to alter the system. My entire purpose in writing the preceding chapter is to make you aware of the real nature of the system. You as an individual will have little hope of changing it, but there is one thing you can do. Armed with this knowledge, you can now begin to protect yourself and your wealth against the inevitable results of the actions going on within the system.

CHAPTER TWO

Plans and Strategies

The retention of part of the efforts of your labor is called the accumulation of wealth. If you can't understand what is likely to happen in the economy of the nation and the world, it would be impossible to adequately protect your stored wealth against loss. At this point, you should have an understanding of real economics, and armed with this, you should be on your way to predicting the future. The next step in developing a rational strategy for accumulating wealth is to develop your goals. This is something that most never do, and the few that do, frequently go about it improperly.

GOALS—

It's hard to imagine that you would set sail in a boat without a firm destination in mind. It's also hard to imagine that you would begin construction of a house without knowing what kind you intended to complete or what size you wanted. Yet, this is precisely what you are doing when you start to accumulate wealth without knowing how much you are after, and when you want to reach the goal. In every facet of our lives, we seem to know the value of planning. We plan our destination when we leave on vacation; we plan an inventory when we stock our business; we plan the menu before preparing dinner. But in the most difficult of all achievements, that of becoming independently wealthy, we

assume that planning is unnecessary and we never give it a
thought. Oh, for sure you might decide that you'd like to
have a million dollars, or that you might like to make as
much as you can. But that's not planning. You're about as
likely to achieve reasonable success that way as you are if
you set sail for Hawaii without a compass.

How does one set goals in an economy that is as erratic as
ours, and what should a goal be in the first place? To start
with, think about wealth itself, and your primary needs in
life. We work to survive: to eat, provide shelter, and clothes.
After survival is assured, we work to provide comfort and
luxuries. Right now you are enjoying the consumption and
use of a certain amount of products and services every year.
If you added up the food you and your family eat, the
clothes you buy, the use of the home you live in, the
vacations you take and all the other commodities and services
you enjoy, this would be your standard of living. It could be
measured in the amount of dollars it would take to purchase
these items. Circumstances may occur in your life wherein
you will no longer wish to continue to produce a product for
trade, or may no longer be able to. But the need to eat, be
sheltered and clothed will continue, so your needs will have
to come from your stored wealth. How much wealth you
need to store away will depend on two things: how much do
you consume each year (standard of living), and how many
years will you still be consuming.

There are three situations in which you need to live off
stored wealth:

1. *You may live to retirement age.* If you live,
you may decide not to work any more in order to do
something you value more, i.e., fish, travel, go back
to school, devote your time to charity or politics, etc.
Statistically, it is most likely that you'll live a
relatively healthy life until sometime between age 70
and 80. Assuming you will tire of pursuing your
profession somewhere between age 50 and 65, there
is an unknown span of years (perhaps as few as

fifteen; perhaps as many as forty) during which you'll want to maintain a comfortable living standard without being pressed to regularly produce and sell a service or product. The only replacement for your regular working income must be your wealth, so you must either store up enough to last, or store up enough so that the income from this wealth will replace the income you received from working.

2. *You may die before you accumulate enough wealth to replace your income.* In this case, the question arises, "who will be affected if your income doesn't continue?" If you're the breadwinner, married and supporting a family, that family will now be without support. Assuming the spouse is not equipped to provide support, then the accumulated wealth must provide it. If there is not enough of that, then there is one other solution; life insurance. Life insurance can provide the lump sum of capital that is necessary to continue the income stream uninterrupted, and can replace the sum of capital you would have accumulated if you had lived, worked and saved. In the chapter on life insurance I'll go into depth on how to integrate your life insurance requirements with your over-all planning and how to buy the right policy.

3. *You may become unable to produce income due to a disabling sickness or accident.* In this case, the income from your present accumulated assets may not be enough to maintain your standard of living and you may be forced to quickly consume those assets and wind up relying on charity for sustenance. A serious risk, without question. Here again disability income insurance can help to cover this risk until you are able to accumulate enough wealth to replace your income. In the chapter on Disability Insurance, I'll cover the why, when and how of its purchase.

Since in all three situations (retirement, death and disabili-

ty) the need is for a continuing income, step one in setting a
financial goal is to determine what standard of living you feel
is adequate, measured by *today's* dollars. To do this, make
out a monthly budget. Figure 6 is an example of a budget
form that could be used. The first objective is to determine
the permanent monthly income that will satisfy your needs.
You can consider yourself independently wealthy when you
have enough capital so that the income from the capital will
meet these needs.

If someone told you that they were willing to send you a
check every month for the rest of your life, and they would
adjust the amount of the check to the cost of living increase
every year, what would the amount of that check have to be
to cover your living expenses? Figure 6 is a sample monthly
budget which tallies current expenses, expenses in the event
of death of the breadwinner, and expenses in the event of his
disability. You'll find a blank for your use in the Appendix.
As you determine what your present expenses are, you
should realize that certain expenses would cease if you
suddenly had a permanent income. For example, you would
no longer need life insurance, for the purpose of life
insurance is really just to replace the breadwinner's earning
power anyway. Furthermore, you would no longer need
disability insurance, either. Payments on investment
property, dollar cost averaging into stocks, and retirement
plan deductions from your income would no longer be
necessary. You would still have to pay income taxes, of
course, but don't consider them at this point as there is a way
to adjust for them later. You should figure in a reserve for
replacement of "wasting" assets, that is a fund to replace
things that wear out, such as automobiles, clothes, furniture,
etc. Figure out your budget and determine the total amount
of income you'll need every month.

For the sake of discussion, let's assume that you decide
$1,500 per month of today's dollars is adequate to maintain
a comfortable standard of living.

SAMPLE MONTHLY BUDGET

	Current	After Death of Spouse	If Disabled
Regular Expenses			
Mortgage or Rent	$ 230	$ 230	$ 230
Utilities	50	40	40
Maid, Gardener, Pool Service, etc.	30	50	40
Groceries, Milk, Liquor	275	200	275
Lunches	40	20	20
Entertainment, Meals, Shows, etc.	80	50	80
Recreation (Skiing, Boating, etc.)	50	40	40
Clothes	150	100	150
Laundry, Cleaning, Shoe Repair	20	20	20
Personal (Haircuts & Allowances)	100	50	100
Auto Operation (Gas, Tires, Repairs)	100	50	50
Tuitions, Lessons	20	20	20
Donations	20	10	10
Support of Others, Alimony, etc.	—	—	—
Auto Loans (Or Amortization)	100	80	80
Other Loans	135	—	135
Total Regular Expenses	$1,400	$ 960	$1,300
Periodic Expenses			
Real Estate Taxes	$ 60	$ 60	$ 60
Household Maintenance & Repair	50	75	75
New Household Purchases	50	50	50
Casualty Insurance (Auto, Home)	40	30	30
Life Insurance	50	—	50
Disability, Medical Insurance	70	40	40
Vacations	100	75	100
Gifts (Birthdays, Anniv., Xmas)	50	30	50
Income Taxes, State & Federal	350	100	100
Legal, Accounting	10	10	10
Medical, Dental, Veterinarian	20	20	—
Total Periodic Expenses	$ 850	$ 490	$ 585
Savings & Investments			
Real Estate	$ 40	$ —	$ 40
Securities	100	—	100
Miscellaneous	25	—	25
Total Savings & Investments	$ 165	$ —	$ 165
Total Monthly Expenses	$2,415	$1,450	$2,050

Figure 6

The question is, how much capital would be needed to provide that income? It will depend, of course, on the rate of return you receive on the invested capital. $1,500 per month is $18,000 per year. A little simple arithmetic will tell you that if you had $360,000 in a bank account and the bank was paying you 5% per year interest, then that interest would amount to $18,000 per year. You'd be sadly disappointed if you stopped there, however. The government would step in and take a portion of the $18,000 for taxes (probably around $3,000) and you would wind up with only $15,000 to live on. Next year prices would go up also. You would find that what costs $18,000 today might cost $19,000 or $20,000 next year. So between taxes and inflation, you'd quickly find that $360,000 yielding 5% would not meet your needs. Your choices would be to:

1. Increase the rate of return;
2. Increase the amount of capital;
3. Use up some of the capital each year.

TRUE RATE OF RETURN—

This brings us into a discussion of what I call True Rate of Return. When a bank pays interest on normal passbook savings accounts, it pays somewhere around 5% per annum. This is an apparent rate of return, for although the bank may pay you 5%, the government is going to tax that interest. The percentage they'll take depends on the level of your income. In addition to this, your capital will be losing its purchasing power at the rate of inflation, whatever that may be. The True Rate of Return then would be the Apparent Rate of Return less Income Taxes and less the Current Rate of Inflation.

Assuming you'd like to accumulate sufficient capital to provide yourself with an income of $18,000 per year (adjusted for inflation), you can calculate the amount of capital you'll need, provided you know the apparent rate of return you'd be getting on your investments. One thing becomes quickly evident. If the rate of inflation is 10% and your tax bracket is 30%, then you're going to have to get a pretty hefty *apparent* rate of return (14.3%) before you'll be able to realize *any* positive True Rate of Return. You are now being exposed to one of the great fallacies of the investment industry; the idea that compound interest will make you rich. How many times have I heard investment salesmen tell their prospects that if they put away $100 a month from age 35 to 65 at some nominal rate of return like 10%, they'll wind up rich. The salesman will show you a compound interest table and point out that just $100 per month will accumulate to be $217,000 at that rate. What will it be on a true scale? If your combined tax bracket were only 30% and inflation averaged 4%, then you would accumulate purchasing power of only $58,000, a far cry from the amount promised; and if your bracket is 60% (which only requires a $32,000 taxable income for a single resident of California) and if the inflation rate is 10% (and I'll be amazed if it can be held to that) you'll wind up at age 65 with enough purchasing power to buy only $16,700 worth of goods and services by today's standards. That's less purchasing power than the amount saved! You not only won't get wealthy using compound interest coupled with regular savings, you'll probably lose money!

Unfortunately, the miscalculation perpetrated by the investment salesman will not be noticed until years and years later, and even then it's unlikely that the victim will relate his economic plight to the original error in strategy. He'll just realize it didn't work out, and he can't make it in retirement. Nothing more aptly illustrates this than rereading the insurance ad that used to run in national magazines. It showed a picture of a smiling man holding aloft a freshly caught fish. "My wife and I retired in Florida on $129.00 a month, thanks to our Phoenix Mutual Insurance Policy." A vivid reminder of the devastation of inflation that must surely haunt the people at Phoenix Mutual.

In today's economy I would think any person both shrewd and fortunate who can achieve a positive true rate of return on capital which is passively invested. Inflation ran at an annual rate of 12% during 1974. This means anyone in a 50% tax bracket would have to have earned at least 24% on his investments just to break even! Even trying to project what inflation might be in the future is futile. In planning for retirement, suppose I assume that inflation will be 10% per year 20 years from now when I want to begin drawing off my wealth, and I adjust my goal accordingly. What if the rate winds up at 15%, or 30%? All my planning has been worthless. Somehow it's necessary to develop a strategy that does not depend on projecting the rate of inflation, and that is done by using True-Rate-of-Return. Here's a sample calculation:

Retirement Income Needed $18,000
Number of Years of Retirement 25
True Rate of Return Assumed Possible .. 0%

$18,000 x 25 years = $450,000

Your goal then will be reached when you have accumulated $450,000 in dollars by today's standards. If you had $450,000 this year and you could get 0% true rate of return, you could stop working now and have a permanent income of $18,000 per year *of today's dollars* for the next 25 years. Since dollars next year or ten years from now will have less purchasing power, it will be necessary to have more of them to have the equivalent of $450,000. You may find that prices go up so much that you might need $5 million, and at 4% that would yield $200,000 per year, but inflation may have caused prices to rise so much that it would cost that $200,000 per year to buy the same goods and services that $18,000 will buy today. Since you are making the assumption that you can earn 0% true, your total capital will be going up even though its purchasing power isn't. Does it sound fantastic that your living expenses could go to $200,000 per year? Impossible? Remember when bread cost 5 cents a loaf? Did it seem possible that it could ever cost 50 cents? Don't kid yourself. It could go to $5 a loaf. It could go to $50 a loaf. It could go to $5,000 a loaf.

A rational financial goal, then, is one in which the amount of capital accumulated will provide a continuation of an acceptable standard of living for as long as you may live. Since most people will be very fortunate to break even on their investments, let alone get any positive true-rate-of-return, you might as well figure on accumulating enough wealth to last for the amount of time you figure on living. For example, if you think you'll live twenty years past retirement, and your current living expenses are $15,000 per year, figure on accumulating 20 years x $15,000 or $300,000. Then if your return on the capital is enough to meet inflation and taxes, your money will last you the length of time you expect to live. If you're fortunate enough to get a true rate of return of 2%, then you'll wind up at the end of twenty years with a little left over for your heirs.

RISK VS. REWARD

> "If you would become wealthy, then what you save must earn, and its children must earn, that all may help give you the abundance you crave."[15]
> (George S. Clason, *The Richest Man In Babylon*)

The purpose of putting your money to work is two-fold. First to preserve the capital for future use. Second to hopefully make that capital increase in size. To examine these two purposes let's take them one at a time. The question of preservation is one of risk. Will my capital be there and be available when I want to consume it five years, or twenty years from now? Or will it be lost due to some risk? The increase of the capital possible through loaning it or investing it also brings up the question of reward. What rate of return can be expected from different types of investments? In other words, what are the risks and what are the rewards?

Most authors writing on the subject of investments tie the two concepts together in what might be called a risk-reward spectrum, generally conceding that the higher the reward sought, the higher must be the risk endured.

The reasoning is clear. Money has a value. When you offer your money in the marketplace, a number of people will bid for it. The more risky the venture, the more that venture will have to pay for the use of your money. A person bidding for your money will want to get it as cheaply as he can; he'll want to give away as little of his future profit from his business venture as possible in return for the use of the capital. If he could borrow the money on the credit of his venture with a promise to repay at the minimum interest available, that's what he would do. Barring his ability to do this, then he'll raise the amount of interest he's willing to pay higher and higher until at last he "bids" your capital away from the other venturers that are offering their investments and loans in the market. He may offer to borrow your money with a promise to repay at some later date, with interest. Or he may actually sell you an interest in his business, which would include a share of the profits and losses as well as an ownership in present assets. He might combine the two by offering a loan and the opportunity to convert the loan into a share of the business later. In any case, he won't bid any more for your money than absolutely necessary, and you'll shop the market to determine that his is the best offer around. This is what gives rise to the concept that risk increases as reward increases.

RISK

Another word that has come up over and over again in our discussion is *risk*. Risk means exposure to loss. You'll never have a good grasp of handling money and accumulating wealth unless you can isolate and identify the variety of risks that face you. To most of us, the primary risk that we consider

when making investment decisions is the risk of loss due to the
market value of our investment falling. Many "conservative"
older folks who suffered the market crash of 1929 won't have
anything to do with investing in stocks due to the risk of
another depression. This is far from the most important or the
only risk that must be avoided. I break risks down into two
categories. The first are what I call *economic* risks, or those
risks of loss due to general economic conditions outside the
control of myself or the management of the companies in
which I invest. The second group of risks are what I term
financial risks, or those risks of loss due to poor selection,
timing, or planning on my part. Risks that fall into the
economic category are as follows:

INFLATION—the risk that a general rise in prices will
decrease my purchasing power;

RUNAWAY INFLATION—Same as inflation, only the
rise in prices gets out of control, as it did in France in
1789, and in Germany in 1913-1923;

RECESSION—The risk that my assets will lose value
due to a slow down in business activity and lower
profits for industry;

DEPRESSION—The risk that my assets will lose value
because of widespread industrial collapse and unemployment;

SOCIALISM—The risk that my assets will lose value
due to confiscation by the government or by restrictions on the use or transfer of those assets;

WAR—Risk of physical destruction or capture.

Risks that fall in the Financial category are as follows:

BUSINESS FAILURE—The risk that I will invest in a
business that fails due to bad management or other
internal miscalculations;

FRAUD—The risk that I will be defrauded of my
assets;

NATURAL DISASTER—The risk that my assets will
be wiped out by a natural disaster such as flood, fire,
accident, sickness, premature death, etc.;

POOR TIMING—The risk that I'll lose due to buying
my investments at the high point on the price cycle,
and being forced to sell them after they've dropped;
THEFT—The risk that my assets will be stolen.

You may be able to think of other risks that face you in
handling your assets. Those above are, in my opinion, the
most critical. Unfortunately, there is no one way to protect
against all the risks, but we can break protection against loss
down into a couple of categories: methods of physically
protecting the assets, and methods of selecting the appropri-
ate asset that inherently protects against a given risk.
Different types of assets protect against different risks, which
is an obvious reason for diversification. Common stocks are
generally accepted protection against the risk of loss of
purchasing power due to creeping inflation, but a poor
protection against the risk of depression. Cash in the bank
would be a good protection against theft, but a poor
protection against inflation. Figure 7 will give some organization to the way that the different investments relate to the
different risks.

Recognition of the elements of risk is absolutely essential
to construction of a sound strategy for accumulating wealth.
You will be the ultimate judge of which risks are most
imminent, and which, therefore, to defend against most
strongly. One general rule is to always remain as liquid as is
consistent with achievement of your goals. If a choice
presents itself between acquiring an asset that has a wide and
immediate market, and another that would take time and
effort to sell, choose the most readily marketable. Economic,
as well as financial conditions can change rapidly, and as they
do it's necessary to shift your portfolio accordingly. If we
head rapidly into runaway inflation or a depression, you may
be unable to find buyers for certain non-liquid assets such as
income real estate, art, stock of closely held companies,
limited partnerships, etc. The chances of growth from these
types of investments must be weighed against the risks
inherent in their lack of liquidity.

Risk/Protection

	RISKS TO WEALTH	PROTECTION				
		STORES OF VALUE	LOANS	EQUITIES	Speculations	OTHER
ECONOMIC	Inflation	2	3	2	3	Liquidity.
	Hyper-Inflation	1	4	3	2-3	Liquidity.
	Recession	2	2	3	3	Liquidity.
	Depression	2	3	4	4	Liquidity.
	Socialism	2	3	3		Liquidity; Concealed Foreign Accounts.
FINANCIAL	Business Failure	1	2	3	4	Diversification; Conservatism.
	Fraud	1	2	3	3	Knowledge; Control; Conservatism.
	Taxation	1	3	2	2	Form of Ownership.
	Poor Timing	1	2	3	3	Dollar-Cost Averaging.
	Spendthrift	3	2	2		Discipline.
	Personal Catastrophe	1	2	2	3	Liquidity; Insurance.

KEY: 1 VERY GOOD
      2 GOOD
      3 BAD
      4 VERY BAD

Figure 7

WHEN IS A "SAVINGS ACCOUNT" REALLY A LOAN?

A proper understanding of investment theory must start with definitions and categories. Throughout your life you've been exposed to investment terminology, but I wonder if you've ever had a clear understanding of what the words meant, or how they related to one another. Loans, equities, speculations, gambles. The confusion about the meanings of these words has resulted in a lot of misdirected programs and much of the confusion comes directly from the financial world in the form of camouflage. For example, one tends to put "saving" in a lower risk category than "lending." Consequently, the banker will tell you to "save" at his bank rather than ask you to "lend" him your money, even though loaning him your money is exactly what you're doing when you deposit it in his "savings account." The commodities broker will ask you to "invest" in commodities futures, feeling that if he asked you to "speculate" it wouldn't seem so secure. The life insurance company will ask you to "invest" in cash value life insurance, or "buy a piece of the rock," insinuating that you have equity ownership in the company itself, or that you in some way participate in the profits they receive from their investments. In reality, it's not an investment at all, but a straight loan to the life insurance company. It's no wonder that there is confusion over the investment terminology when the industry itself works so hard at altering the image of its products.

The first step in organizing your investment program is to be able to recognize the true nature of any asset that is offered you. There are four things that you can do with your money. All types of offerings fall into one of these categories.

Store of Value: The first thing you can do with your excess production is to *store* it. If you're an apple farmer you can keep your extra apples in the cellar, for use at a later time. Or you can trade them for hides, wheat, chairs, or whatever other commodity you think will be usable later, and store that. A store-of-value asset is a *usable commodity* that is held by the owner for later trade or consumption. Any commodity, therefore, could be a store-of-value asset, but certainly some commodities would be more practical to store and thus would be more useful for this purpose. Fertilizer would be too bulky to store; bananas would spoil; and automobiles would go out of style. The best store-of-value assets are also those assets that would best serve as money. For example, gold and silver are practical store-of-value assets. So are diamonds, art, and raw land. All usable stores of value.

Loans: The second thing you can do with your excess production is to lend it to someone else for their use. The apple farmer could lend the tailor five bushels of apples, with the understanding that next year the tailor would pay him back (with a few apples extra for interest on the use of the money). Most so-called "conservative" investors use loans as their primary vehicle for accumulating wealth. You can lend your money to a friend, to a bank, to a savings and loan company, to a life insurance company, to a corporation, and to a state. In all these cases, you are given a promise of repayment called a note or a bond. That is, a promise to repay with interest at a specified future date, or on demand. Different loans carry different rates of interest, and of course, different degrees of risk based on the financial integrity of the borrower.

Equities: The third thing that you can do with your money is to buy ownership or part ownership of some type of a business enterprise. You could buy a service station or a grocery store, alone or in partnership with others. This use of money would include owning shares of stock in corporations and owning income producing real estate. An apartment building, for example, is a (hopefully) profit-making business, as is a vineyard and a warehouse. Most equities include some of the attributes of store-of-value assets in that almost always a business must own some commodities; i.e., income producing real estate usually includes land, the grocery store includes groceries, and industrial corporations include equipment.

Gambling: The fourth and last thing that can be done with your wealth is to gamble with it. Gambling simply means placing a wager that a certain event will happen. It differs from the other categories in that no ownership is involved; the event will be purely a matter of chance, and you can therefore have no foreknowledge of its occurrence.

SPECULATION

No discussion of money use would be complete without covering that usually fuzzy area called "speculation." The dictionary defines speculation as "buying and selling with a view to making profits from future price changes." Unfortunately, this definition would mean that all investments, as we've defined them, would be speculations, and for our purposes, this isn't necessarily correct. When used in this book, speculation is defined as the purchase of any thing in belief that the *supply/demand forces* in the market will cause its price to rise. Thus, if I buy a stock not with the intention of holding that stock in order to profit from the future growth of the company or the current earnings of the company, but solely because I believe that the stock is currently underpriced and soon the market will discover this and the price will rise accordingly, then I am speculating. In the same way, if I buy any commodity, like gold for example, with the idea that the demand for gold is going to get greater and thus bid up the price, then I am speculating on the future supply/demand factors for that commodity, not buying it simply as a store of value. You can even speculate with loans by buying bonds, not with the intention of holding those bonds for the income, but because you believe that interest rates will drop and make your bonds more valuable.

Throughout the investment industry, market values of all commodities and investments are driven up and down by the forces of speculation; but the underlying values of store-of-value assets, equities, and loans are what must ultimately be looked to when developing a rational strategy for accumulating wealth. The speculative market is a big poker game with each player hoping to profit from the other players' mistakes. The rational market, on the other hand, is a market in which one person's profit is not dependent on another person's mistakes. The thing that should be realized is that the speculative market is superimposed over the rational market. There is a level at which the price of commodities and businesses should rest. That is, they should be priced at what they could be duplicated for by the efforts of other labor, capital, and thought. In the commodities and stock markets you can watch the prices of commodities and stocks fluctuate above and below the price they will eventually bring on the real market as they are successively under-priced and over-priced by speculators. Most of us are not equipped to be speculators anymore than most of us are equipped to sit down with professional poker players and walk away winners. We should try to find the natural levels, and place our funds into store-of-value, loans and equities based on a long run conservative strategy and a sound knowledge of the underlying economic conditions

Speculation then, is not the thing that you're buying, but the way that you're buying it. Raw land purchased because you think land will become more valuable due to increasing population is purchased as a speculation. Raw land purchased because you want to put your money in a commodity that will retain its relative value in the face of depreciating purchasing power of dollars is a store-of-value asset. Gold purchased because you believe a devaluation is imminent is a speculation. Gold purchased because you think it will be a commodity that will hold its trading value in the face of inflation is a store-of-value asset. These distinctions are going to be extremely important as we get into the chapters on selection of types of assets for your portfolio, and it is well that you understand them.

MARGINING OR MORTGAGING

It's a sad fact of life that almost all human decisions are based on either emotion or hearsay. This is never more true than in the question of borrowing money to invest. Should I pay off my home mortgage? Should I buy silver on margin? If I buy an apartment house for income, how large a mortgage should I seek? Should stocks be margined? Should I pay cash for new equipment for my plant or office?

You have been confronted with this question time after time and your answer was probably based on some personal prejudice (stories or experiences from the depression, for example). Stanford University economist G.L. Bach points out that young families who never experienced the depression have large debts, payable later in cheaper dollars.[14] The old, remembering the trauma of the 30's, have few debts and comparatively large holdings in such low interest monetary assets as savings accounts. What are the pro's and con's of going into debt?

There are two situations in which a person might borrow money. First, if you haven't yet produced enough to allow you to trade for something you want, then you may go on the line for your future earnings in order to have that desired item now. An example would be a young couple who can't afford to pay cash for a car, so they borrow the money to buy one and pay off the loan a few dollars every month. Second, you may borrow to purchase investment assets; these are not consumed but are bought to increase your wealth.

Borrowing For Consumption

As far as borrowing money to buy a higher standard of living (i.e., a new refrigerator, etc.), you are merely sentencing yourself to a lower standard of living in the long run. While you may enjoy the use of the refrigerator, the interest you pay will not be available to buy other items that would additionally increase your comfort. The person who waits to buy his conveniences until he can pay cash is always better off. In addition, borrowing for consumption robs you of your freedom of choice. Not only do you wind up with a lower standard of living, once in debt, you must make all decisions based on whether or not the choice will interfere with your ability to repay your loans. Your creditors sit in on every decision you make. You may want to move to a new environment, take a more interesting but lower paying job, or take time for leisure, but your creditors prohibit it. We are a nation built, supposedly, on consumer credit, yet I maintain it has done more to hold back the standard of the nation than anything other than the government. My advice is simple in regards to consumption items: pay cash.

Borrowing For Investment

There are a variety of reasons one might give for borrowing for investment. If you borrow money to buy a car in order to get a job that requires a car, then there is reason. If I'm a dentist and have no money to equip my office unless I borrow, then I'll borrow in order to earn. These are forms of borrowing to increase the capacity to earn, and is done on a massive scale by both individuals and industry. Your decision on whether to borrow for investment, whether it be in your own business or in some other asset, should be weighed against two considerations. First, economics. Is it financially profitable? That can be fairly easily determined by comparing the after-tax cost of the financed product with the after-tax return of the dollars invested. It will depend on your tax bracket, the cost of financing the product, and the type and amount of projected return on your invested funds.

The second and often overlooked consideration is risk. How sure are you that you can continue to receive the stated income on your investment during the length of time you'll be paying off the loan? How sure can you be that you'll be in a position to continue to make the principal payments on the loan? If something goes wrong and you're unable to continue making the payments, will you be able to liquidate your investment in order to pay off the loan? If so, would you possibly have to liquidate at a loss in order to prevent foreclosure? Take a hypothetical example: you have ten thousand dollars. You would like to buy a boat, and plan to charter it for income. Instead of buying for cash, you finance on a five year note at 6% add-on interest, and put your money in a savings and loan and draw 6% interest, drawing on the principal to make the payments. If your economic situation doesn't change, everything can be predicted. But what would happen if the country slid into a depression six months after you made the deal? Well, you probably wouldn't be able to get your money out of the savings and loan. They have taken your money and put it into long term trust deeds and might not be able to retrieve it. Your lender, however, would insist that you continue to make your payments on the boat. If you couldn't charter it, you'd have to turn to your personal income, which may or may not be available, to make the payments. The right set of circumstances could mean you'd lose the boat.

The risk is there, and if it doesn't seem real, talk to the hundreds of thousands of people who went bankrupt during the last depression when they watched their assets melt away in building and loans, or banks that went bankrupt, while they themselves were unable to meet the mortgages they were carrying. Money in the bank isn't all as safe as one might think. The reason people borrow for investments is to increase the rate of return over what they could get if they paid cash. Only in the case where the increased return is due to tax savings will you find your risk not increased, and even then it could be. Margining is risky. In a depression, prices of all commodities fall, including the commodities you hold or produce, but loan balances do not fall.

An example of this risk is the recent experience of many investors in the real estate market. In 1969, there was a general drop in stock prices, and consequently, many investors were scared out of the stock market. There were very low vacancy factors at the time in the residential housing market so many turned towards apartment house syndications for tax savings and growth. By putting down as low as 10% of the purchase price, they could buy an apartment building (most pooled their money in large syndications). Assuming a 5% vacancy factor, the income from the project would be enough to carry the mortgages, expenses of operation, and pay a small cash flow to the owner. Everything was fine until the economy slumped and vacancies began to increase. Suddenly there wasn't enough cash from rentals to cover mortgage payments and operating costs, and unless the investors were financially prepared to subsidize the apartments on a monthly basis, it was foreclosure time. Thousands of real estate projects went into foreclosure during the period from 1970 to 1973, and it wasn't because of a general

depression. Just a slump in real estate occupancy did
the trick.

The same considerations hold true in the stock market as
in the real estate market, with a couple of exceptions. In real
estate, loans are generally made for a long term at a fixed
monthly payment; if the price of real estate falls, the banker
can't suddenly call his loan or ask for more margin. In stocks
the price is quoted daily on the exchange and consequently a
banker can look at his margin loan at any time and determine
whether there is sufficient equity in the account to cover his
risk. If the value of a stock falls, he may ask for more
collateral (known as a margin call). If you don't have the
capital to meet the margin calls, you lose your equity. The
purpose of margining in the market is to leverage your capital
to increase your profits. If you're wrong, you increase your
losses by the same leverage by which you would have
increased your gains.

A second risk that exists in margining stocks: when you
buy on margin you don't have the stock certificates in your
hands. Even if the stocks did appreciate, you still have to rely
on the financial integrity of the brokerage house. Considering
the number of firms that have failed in the last few years, this
must be a significant risk.

There is little difference between margining stocks and
margining commodities. I might buy stocks, silver, gold coins,
wheat, or pork bellies and the factors of margining don't
change. In either case I get only a receipt so I must rely on
the integrity of the broker; I'm subject to margin calls; I
increase my reward if I'm right, and my loss if I'm wrong.

The ultimate question is, *"what rate of return do you need
to get on your investments?"* Why go after the higher rates and
subject yourself to the increased risks, if you don't really
need that increased rate of return to meet your goals? There
we are back to goals again. The *goal* is the determining factor.

CHAPTER THREE

Selecting a Rational Portfolio

This chapter will familiarize you with most of the things you can buy as a method of storing or increasing your wealth. The purpose is not to make specific recommendations but rather to define the advantages and disadvantages of each asset in relation to your particular goals and relative to the risks, both economic and financial. There is no investment that can be guaranteed to preserve or increase your wealth; only in given economic conditions some investments are *more likely* to enable you to reach your goals than others. Never look for a panacea: recognize that you must diversify, and that you must be prepared to change your portfolio completely as times and conditions change.

STORE-OF-VALUE

Earlier I defined store-of-value assets as usable commodities that are held by the owner for later trade or consumption, and pointed out that any commodity could be used for this purpose. Now you should begin to see a definite correlation between a store-of-value asset and what was earlier defined as *money*. Money, as you may recall, was any commodity that was taken in exchange with the intention of holding it and later trading it for something that was to be consumed. A store-of-value asset is almost identical. Almost, but not exactly. With money the real idea is the "exchange" idea, and the length of time the commodity is held is of minor significance. With store-of-value assets, the primary consideration is the time factor. How long is it to be held before being traded? A week? Twenty years? Two hundred years? Money's attributes are divisibility, durability, recognized value, and constant supply. Store-of-value assets, on the other hand, do not necessarily have to be divisible (raw land, for example), but they should have all the other attributes of money. They should retain their value relative to other commodities for long periods (which money substitutes never do), and should be recognized for their value (although not necessarily by everyone, as not everyone, for example, would recognize the value of a great work of art). Their supply should not suddenly increase, leading to a loss of trading power in relation to other commodities. In order to minimize storage costs it would be helpful for a small amount of the asset to be worth a great deal.

The purpose of holding store-of-value assets is to preserve the purchasing power of accumulated surplus. An apple farmer may have two bushels of apples left at the end of the season. By trading them for store-of-value assets he should be able to trade back for the two bushels of apples ten years in the future when he decides that it's time to consume those apples. If you could only recognize the immense difficulty of this feat you'd come a lot closer to accomplishing it.

All store-of-value assets are affected in a similar way by economic conditions. In a slowly inflating economy they tend to rise slowly in value, keeping pace with inflation. In a hyper-inflating society they again tend to hold their value, as they are the yardstick by which the declining value of the currency is being measured. In a recession they tend to hold their value relative to each other. In a depression they hold their value relative to other commodities, but may lose their value relative to money or money substitutes. I said *may*, for depending on what is happening to the money supply at the time, they may still be rising in price.

The balance of this chapter will be devoted to a discussion of some of the more common store-of-value assets.

GOLD

In the last half of the decade of the 1940's the natural element most on men's minds was uranium. In the last half of this decade the element will be gold. For almost forty years the government of the United States has succeeded in eradicating the question of the value of gold from the minds of the masses simply by offering to sell it at $35 per ounce. In 1971, its vaults nearly exhausted, Uncle Sam at last had to admit that he could no longer supply the commodity at that price.

People abroad were placing their wealth in American dollars under the belief that these really represented claims on gold and that holding them was as good as holding gold. By 1971 the total outstanding claims on gold held overseas were almost $100 billion. Yet the total supply of gold in the U.S. Treasury was only 291 million ounces; at $35 an ounce, $10.2 billion. The stock was sufficiently low that it could have been wiped out in one day, and rather than let that happen, on August 15, 1971 Nixon suspended the convertibility of dollars held by foreigners into gold the same as Roosevelt had done for American citizens some 38 years earlier. On December 18, 1971 he devalued the dollar in relation to gold from $35 per ounce to $38 per ounce.

Since foreign banks could no longer redeem dollars for gold, devaluation seemed a meaningless action as it only dealt with the central banks and the price at which they could sell their gold. The devaluation did have a significant effect on the money supply of the U.S., however, as it increased the official dollar value of treasury gold holdings by $800 million and thus allowed the treasury to buy $800 million of goods and services from the private sector of the economy. This $800 million, once in the banking system,

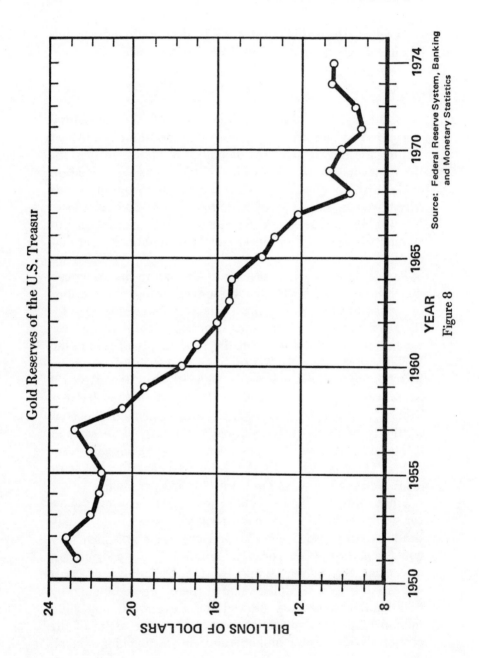

Gold Reserves of the U.S. Treasur

Source: Federal Reserve System, Banking and Monetary Statistics

YEAR

Figure 8

BILLIONS OF DOLLARS

supported a $2 billion higher level of the money stock.*

After the suspension of redemption and the first devaluation the price of gold in the free market jumped from $35 per ounce to about $65 per ounce. In February of 1973 Nixon again was faced with massive balance of payments deficits and a declining dollar value on world money markets. He chose to devalue again, this time pegging the price of gold at $42.22 (a ficticious price only applicable to central banks). This again resulted in a bonanza for the treasury, giving them $1.2 billion of new spending power. At this point the free market price of gold jumped to $100 and then rose to a high point in 1973 of $130 per ounce. From there the balance of payments position of the United States seemed to begin to stabilize, and the free market price of gold drifted down to the $100 per ounce range. In November of 1973 the six countries that make up the gold block nations met and agreed that they should no longer be held to selling their reserves only at the price of $42.22 per ounce, but should be allowed to sell at will at the free market price. The price dropped from around $100 down to $90, in that speculators feared one or more of the central banks might decide to dump gold into the free market and cause a collapse of gold prices. Within a week or two, however, rumors that the Arabs might demand gold in payment for much needed oil again brought the price up to $100 an ounce, and from there it moved up relentlessly to a high in 1974 of about $184.

What do these fluctuations mean? Simply that speculators are pushing the price up and down? What should the natural price be, and where will the price go in the future?

Theoretically the price of gold will be a result of supply and demand pressures. Let's take a brief look at these two factors.

---

*This effect is discussed at length in an article by Albert E. Burger, "The Monetary Economics of Gold", in the January, 1974 *Review* of the Federal Reserve Bank of St. Louis.

Supply—

Supply can come from several sources:

1. Free world central banks. They currently hold about 980 million ounces or $147 billion worth at $150 per ounce.

2. Private hoarders. It is estimated that private citizens and corporations hold approximately 700 million ounces or $105 billion worth.

3. New mining. Experts estimate that approximately 50 million ounces of gold are currently being mined annually. Of course, as the price of gold on the free market increases, gold production will increase. Mines that were uneconomical to exploit at $35 per ounce might be very profitable at $150 per ounce. It has been only three years since the price broke from $35 per ounce and the development of new mines takes far longer than that, so the world production figures have not had an opportunity to reflect the increased price for the metal.

Demand

What about demand? The question of the value of gold, as with the value of any commodity, is: will demand be greater than supply, or vice versa? Unlike most commodities, there are two aspects to demand for gold. The first is industrial demand. Industry, and this includes art, dentistry, electronics, and all other commercial uses, is currently consuming over 40 million ounces per year. My guess is that as the technological revolution proceeds, vast new areas of commercial and scientific uses will appear and consumption will soar. The second aspect of demand is the demand for gold as a store-of-value asset. Over the history of mankind this has certainly been its primary use.

Will the demand for gold as a store-of-value asset increase or decrease in the future? Man has always esteemed gold for its unique properties. It's malleable; it can be hammered into sheets so thin that it takes a stack of 5,000,000 of them to stand an inch high. It can be drawn into a wire so fine that a piece of it 50 miles long would weigh only an ounce.* An object of pure gold can be left in salt water for a thousand years and never lose its luster. It has a rare beauty, being the most beautiful of all metals, and it has always been very difficult to come by. Isn't it hard to imagine that suddenly, just because governments want to rid themselves of the restrictions imposed by a gold monetary standard, that they can dismiss gold's value, and individuals all over the world will no longer desire it? It's not just hard to imagine. It's a rank absurdity to think such a thing.

There is no doubt in my mind that international currency inflation will reach unprecedented heights in the next few years, and the demand of individuals for gold will be greater than ever before. Remember that there are 220 million people in the U.S. who have been restricted from gold ownership. Now that this ban is being lifted a vast new market is opened up. Additionally, these same U.S. citizens are for the first time in their memories being subjected to rampant inflation. This year there may still be $235 billion in savings and loan and $255 billion in life insurance companies, but what will happen when it becomes apparent to these safety conscious investors that inflation is here to stay and their savings are being devastated? They're going to begin looking around for safe havens. Gold will be one answer.

At a market price of $150 per ounce there is only

*For an interesting side trip into the world of gold I highly recommend Timothy Green's The World of Gold Today, Walker and Company, New York, 1973.

$7.5 billion in new gold being mined each year. Weighed against some $976 billion currently tucked away in savings and loans, life insurance companies, and bank savings accounts, that's just a drop in the bucket. What if the governments decide to dump their supplies on the market? Would they do this? Let's examine the psychology that might be at work here. Suppose for a moment that you're a ruler and you have been backing your currency with gold. When would you stop? In the past histories, the country has stopped when it has issued so much currency in the form of demand notes against its gold that it could no longer cover the demands for redemption. At that point it repudiated the gold claims and said they were worth only a fraction of their original gold value or they were not worth gold at all. In order to accomplish this it was almost always necessary to outlaw gold in the marketplace, for if this wasn't done, people would simply start trading in gold and bypass the government's "legal tender" currency. Since the government had to have the monopoly on the currency in order to fund its operation, it couldn't allow the people to trade in some other commodity. Hence, gold becomes illegal.

Anyone of sound mind would rather trade his production for something that would be tradeable for a real store-of-value commodity, like gold, than for a piece of paper that would probably lose its value. Imagine the position of any country that had no hard reserves whatsoever. If it sold all its gold and silver reserves and from that point forward issued paper money, what would the paper money be worth to a foreign manufacturer? Suppose that they are dependent on foreign oil and the Arabs suddenly demand a "hard" commodity in exchange for their oil. Or suppose they are threatened with a war, their hard metal reserves are gone, and they must buy the food and munitions from other countries in order to protect themselves. Would those other nations or individual manufacturers be willing to accept paper currency or notes? Within the nation the citizens have no choice, for they must accept the "legal tender" or suffer imprisonment, and thus the government can always buy local production with its printing press currency. But foreign production is quite another matter. A government must have a supply of hard money with which to negotiate for foreign production at all times. Therefore it is highly unlikely that any nation would willingly divest itself of its bullion reserves. The idea of several nations suddenly doing this is inconceivable.*

If one subscribes to the premise that it is to the advantage of a government to be able to expand its supply of money at will, and it is true that backing currency by any hard commodity like gold makes this difficult, then it must follow that it is to the advantage of government to devise a situation in which they don't have to back their currency. It seems that all governments desire this economic power over their citizens and the big argument among the international money masters is not whether fiat currency is good or bad, but who gets to inflate his the most. No one in this hierarchy is dedicated to sound money. Obviously if they were, they wouldn't be in the hierarchy. The international bankers in the end are the governments themselves with a mask and a few restrictions. They will eventually wind up solving this money problem, and the solution is bound to be at the cost of the individual.

My opinion is that gold will continue to be in demand, the central banks will continue to hold and even increase their reserves of the metal, gold production will rise but not as fast as consumption, and the price of gold will continue to go up, reaching a level of *at least* $300 an ounce by 1976. The

---

*There is one set of circumstances that could negate this reasoning. If in the future the 'one worlders' are successful in merging the governments of all the major nations into one government, then there might be one international monetary unit, and at last it would be possible to allow the central banks to dump their gold supplies and drive the market for gold into a tailspin.

price will fluctuate as does the stock market, but the general
trend will be up. By my calculations the natural price of gold
in an unrestricted, untampered market was between $200
and $250 per ounce at the end of 1974.* The natural price
will rise along with general price increases of other commodities (that is to say, as the money supply is increased, the
value of money will fall in relation to gold as well as all other
commodities). As a store-of-value asset, gold is mandatory for
every rational portfolio. The question is, how to own it?

Buying Gold

There are three ways in which a person can hold gold:
placer gold, bullion, or coins. Placer gold is simply raw,
unprocessed gold direct from nature. It is in the form of
nuggets and small particles, can be held legally by citizens of
the United States, and can be purchased through various
brokers. Unfortunately it's difficult to determine the quality
and exact quantity of this type of gold until it is refined.
Unless you're an expert in the field you might find yourself
stuck with less than you paid for. An additional problem is
that at some point you're going to want to sell your gold, and
you must assume that the person who sold it to you won't be
around to buy it back. Placer gold might present a problem in
that you would have to find someone who would take your
word for its value.

Now that gold bullion is legal for Americans to own, it can
be purchased through a variety of outlets, including some
banks, coin dealers, and bullion exchanges. Bullion can be
purchased in wafers and bars from less than an ounce up to
1,000 ounces (almost 90 pounds). It will generally bear the

---

*This is based on comparing the price of gold at the turn of the century
($20/ounce) to the prices of a number of other raw commodities in-
cluding wheat, corn, iron, copper, etc. Those commodities on the
average have increased 11 times in price. So gold, had it kept pace,
would now sell for about $220 per ounce.

hallmark of the refiner and will have the weight and fineness stamped on the bar. Obviously gold bullion could be adulterated, so when buying, make sure you buy from reliable sources or have the gold assayed.

The third method of buying gold is to purchase gold coins. Earlier regulations against gold ownership exempted coins held for their numismatic value, thus there has been a brisk traffic in gold coins in the U.S. prior to the legalization of gold ownership. Coins have an advantage over bullion in that they are a known weight and fineness. The gold content of common coins can be found in any collectors handbook. Figure 9 lists a few examples of coins and their gold content.

There has been a good deal of counterfeiting of gold coins, and it would be wise to either buy from a reputable source, or have each coin checked. It is relatively easy, using modern equipment, to determine the authenticity of a coin.

Usually coins will sell at somewhat of a premium over the value of their gold content.

GOLD CONTENT OF TEN COMMON COINS

COIN	TROY OZ. (PURE)
United States $20	.9675
United States $10	.48375
Mexican 50 Pesos	1.2056
Mexican 20 Pesos	.4823
Austrian 100 Corona	.9802
Austrian 20 Corona	.1960
British 1 Pound (Sovereign)	.2354
Netherlands 10 Guilders	.1947
South African 2 Rand	.2354
Switzerland 20 Francs	.1867

Figure 9

It's a rare situation when you'll be able to buy these coins for the value of the gold content alone. To start with, when a government mints a coin it charges a premium (called seigniorage) over and above the cost of manufacture. The U.S. twenty dollar gold piece has .9695 ounces of pure (.999 fine) gold in it. Gold was selling at $20.22 an ounce at the time that these coins were being minted, and thus the coin which the government sold for twenty dollars actually contained only $19.56 in gold. South Africa is currently minting about 10% of its gold production into Krugerrands, which it markets at a price about 8% above the gold value of the coins. Seigniorage tends to stay with the coin, and in addition other factors can increase the coins' "numismatic premium", including scarcity of a particular coin, market demand for coins in general, commission charged by the person selling the coins, etc.

You may find yourself getting interested in numismatics in general if you handle many gold coins, as the appeal of their beauty transcends logic. Then you can begin to become a serious collector with an eye for the date of the coin, its condition, its rarity, etc. For the non-numismatically inclined investor, you'll be buying bulk coins. These coins are not particularly rare and are in average condition for that particular coin and date. If you buy American gold coins or British Sovereigns in bulk, you will probably be buying circulated coins as these coins were used for exchange in the early part of the century.

In recent years gold coins, even if freshly minted, are hardly ever exchanged for other commodities in direct barter. They are still minting Mexican 50-Peso coins in Mexico (they're no longer worth 50 pesos, however), but you'll never get one in change when you cash a large bill at a restaurant. They're purchased exclusively by collectors or people who want to use them as store-of-value assets, and consequently will not be circulated. Their condition will probably be U (Uncirculated) or BU (Brilliant Uncirculated). Even when buying in bulk you'll expect that type of condition.

The premium for average coins of a particular mintage over the value of the gold in the coin will vary from day to day. They are, after all, a commodity like any other commodity. Their price will depend on supply and demand for that coin plus the current price of gold. Figure 10 shows the price of three common coins plotted against the daily price of gold over the last year. While the coin price tends to follow closely the gold price, the numismatic premium does vary.

Where do you buy gold coins? Pick up your yellow pages and look under "Coin Dealers." Most of them will have a stock of coins, and many will have teletype services that link them with coin dealers throughout the United States. They'll be able to check prices all over the country, much as the stock broker can check stock prices, and order anything you want. Caution: prices will vary considerably from dealer to dealer, for although they may all have access to similar wholesale prices, they are free to mark up the coins to whatever they think the traffic will bear.

While most coin shops cater primarily to the numismatist and feel themselves lucky when they can snare a well heeled investor, there has recently been an upsurge in coin "exchanges," new companies that have sprung up to satisfy the desire of the investor who wishes to invest substantial amounts of his assets in gold or silver. In addition it's possible to purchase gold coins through various foreign banks, such as through the Swiss Credit Bank, or the Swiss Bank Corporation.

There are three ways in which you can buy gold coins from these retailers. First, you can pay cash and take delivery of the coins. You then have physical possession and must find a way to safely store the coins to protect against the risk of theft. Second, you can pay cash but not take delivery, by asking the dealer you buy from to store them for you. If you're dealing with a Swiss bank I'd think the risk of storing with them is minimal. If you're dealing with anyone else I'd be very cautious. Once you've asked anyone to store your gold, you're relying on the integrity of that party to honor

The Wholesale Price of Gold Bullion vs. Gold Coins

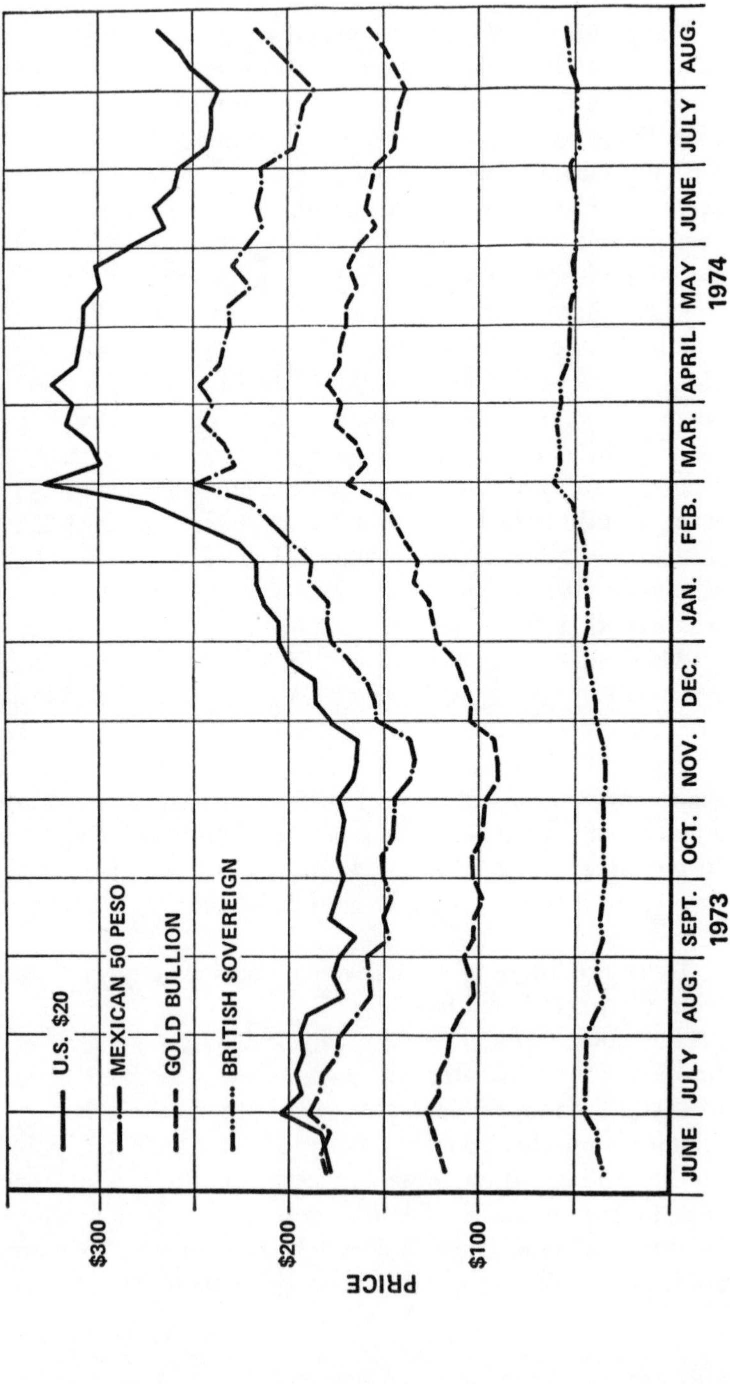

Figure 10

the paper receipt he gives you for your gold. Historically, people who give paper receipts for stored gold have tended to give out more receipts than they have gold on deposit. Isn't that exactly what happened in the case of the U.S. Government? So beware. The third method of buying gold coins is to buy on margin. You purchase a given quantity of coins at the prevailing market price, but put only a small down payment (10% to 20%) on them. You can pick up the coins anytime in the future simply by paying off the balance due, in the meantime paying interest at slightly above the prime rate on the outstanding balance.

The benefits of buying on margin? If the price of gold goes up your coins increase in value. Since you can buy more coins on margin with a given amount of cash than you can buy for delivery, your profit is magnified. Remember the chapter on margining? Using leverage in buying gold coins is not much different than using leverage in the purchase of any other investment. Also, when buying on margin you don't have to worry about taking possession and storing the coins.

What are the risks of buying on margin? First, if the coins go down in value you magnify your loss. Depending on the extent of your leverage, it's easy to have your equity wiped out with a minor downward move in the price of gold. Leveraging or margining is completely inconsistent with the purpose of buying gold, providing your purpose is to hold a store-of-value asset. Secondly, and by far the worst danger, is that the dealer may not put any coins away for you. Suppose I'm a dealer and you buy $10,000 worth of coins from me, paying $1,000 down and agreeing to finance the balance at 8% interest. I give you a contract promising to deliver the coins when the balance is paid off, but who knows whether I really put the coins away or not? If I don't, I now have your $1,000, you pay me interest at the rate of $720 per year, and my cost is nothing. If I'm a "gamblin' man" I might have the feeling that coin prices are going down and plan to buy the coins to cover my obligation to you at some lower price. If the price goes down, I could call for more money from you, as a ten percent drop in price of the coins would wipe out your equity. The profit to me could be substantial. The danger for me and you is that the price of gold could take a substantial jump upwards. In that case I would have to go out and buy the coins I owe you and come up with the difference between what you paid and the new purchase price out of my pocket. On a $10,000 order, if the price of gold jumps 10% then I'll be out of pocket a thousand dollars. A dealer who is trading heavily in coins may process $250,000 worth of orders every week. The temptation to solve short run financial problems by resorting to this tactic is tremendous, and a dealer that succumbs can quickly run up debts in the hundreds of thousands of dollars once any major price move begins. Investors that get caught in this trap find they not only don't have the profits they thought they had, but they've lost their original capital as well.

Margining coins is highly speculative. Know your dealer, and make him prove his claims that he has the gold to back up his contract. But beware again. The fact that he can show you a receipt for gold in the depository isn't enough. What you must know is that he has as much gold as he has receipts outstanding at any time.

A simple remedy for the above discussed dangers is to always buy for cash and take delivery. The profits might not be as high, but neither are the potential losses as great.

Storing Gold

After you have purchased your bullion or coins, you must find a place to keep them. The alternatives are:
  1. A bank safe deposit box.
  2. A wall safe or other hiding place in the home.
  3. A foreign bank safe deposit box.
  4. A non-bank depository.
Your decision should be based on your assessment of the relative risks of each. The possible risks are theft, business

failure, and government confiscation. While bank safe-deposit boxes are relatively theft free they do have a couple of drawbacks. First, the bank could close its doors, in which case it could be awhile before you'd have access to the contents of your box; but even if the bank went through bankruptcy they couldn't get at the contents of your box. Another possibility is that government regulatory agencies such as the IRS or the FBI could gain access to your safe-deposit box without your consent. These agencies have access to all bank records, and a person who fears the confiscatory powers of the state should certainly be aware of the vulnerability of a bank safe-deposit box. Also, in the event of your death the bank is bound by law to notify the taxing authorities of the existence of the box. They'll demand to be present when it's opened in order to tally the value of the contents. If you feel that the state is a potential threat to your wealth, think twice about the use of a bank safe-deposit box for coin storage.

There are non-banking depositories that could serve as alternatives to a banking institution. In most major cities you'll find them listed in the phone book. Typically they are private corporations that own vaults and rent out space in the vaults, usually in the form of lockable boxes, to anyone who wants it. They're usually bonded against theft by the owners, and insured against theft or other loss. Inasmuch as they aren't required to file reports listing their depositors and aren't required to open their vaults to government agents (unless a court order is involved), you have a greater degree of privacy with such an establishment. Foreign banks also rent safe-deposit boxes, and generally Swiss Banks are considered to be safe havens from the prying eyes of neighbors and federal agents.

The final solution is to keep your coins in your own possession. You might bury them in the backyard, build a wall safe into your home (not behind a painting, please!), or simply hide them in some inconspicuous place. The risks you

take here are simple; they could be discovered and stolen by
a thief, melted down from a fire, or possibly scattered to the
winds in a tornado. I know of one couple who kept bags of
silver coins hidden in their home. They found out to their
dismay several months later that neighborhood kids, with
whom they were friendly, had discovered the bags and
gradually pilfered away the coins. Another collector, fearful
of the government, had buried his in the backyard. The coins
survived fine, but he made the mistake of burying several
hundred dollars in Federal Reserve Notes along with them.
When he dug them up he found it was in the nick of time, as
worms had gotten into his box and were busily devouring the
tasty paper. Needless to say, if you're going to stash gold,
silver, or any other valuables on your property, don't talk
about it to anyone. Professional thieves have their ear to the
ground at all times, and they're amazingly adept at dis-
covering the most unlikely hiding places. So be clever and
quiet.

Gold Mining Shares

A fourth method of investing in gold, although somewhat
indirect, is by buying shares of gold mining companies. Gold
is a commodity whose price will fluctuate depending on
supply, demand, and government edict. Since the profits of
companies that mine gold depends directly on the price they
can get for their product, it stands to reason that they will
benefit from an increased price of gold. In fact, the value of
shares of any solid mining company ought to increase at a
much greater rate than the price of gold itself. If a company
is mining gold and it is costing it $30.00 per ounce to mine it,
it will make a $5.00 per ounce profit when it sells the gold at
$35.00 per ounce. If the price rises to $40.00 per ounce the
company has effectively doubled its profits, and if the shares
of stock of the company are consistently selling at some
fixed price-earnings ratio, like 10-1, then doubling the
earnings should effectively double the price of the stock.

Since 1971 the 30 leading South African gold mining stocks have tripled in price. Yet this is nowhere near what they should have done if the rise in the price of gold was translated into earnings increases for those companies. Why? First, in the eyes of the investors, there is no certainty that the price of gold will remain at $150 an ounce or higher. Until the price is officially fixed at or near the free market price, there is no guarantee that the future earnings of the companies will reflect these higher gold prices.

Second, the management of the mines is very conservative. Until they can be assured of a sustained higher price for gold, they won't make the investment in plant and equipment necessary to increase production. In 1934 when the official price of gold was raised to $35 an ounce, it was 3 or 4 years before the mines reached new production levels. Additionally, the earnings of the mines haven't even reflected the increased price of gold based on predevaluation production levels. The management of the mines, uncertain over the future price of gold, began mining lower grade ore bodies when the price increased. Thus they could maintain their old earning levels using ore bodies that couldn't have been profitably mined at the old prices. The higher grade ore could thus be conserved in case the price drops again.

As inflation continues, the price of gold, now a free market commodity, will rise correspondingly. Of course the cost of mining gold will rise as well, partially offsetting the benefits of the increasing gold price. The real benefit to buying gold stocks at this time is that the price of these stocks, as yet, has not reflected the enormous increase in the price of gold, and secondly, gold itself is still underpriced on the world market.

How to buy stocks? You can either make yourself an expert, or rely on some other expert's opinion. Before you do either, you should read Donald J. Hoppe's excellent book, *How to Invest In Gold Stocks and Avoid the Pitfalls.*[15]

If you still don't feel comfortable about following the stocks on a day-to-day basis, choose one of the mutual funds that specialize in gold mining shares. International Investors, Inc. was the first major gold fund. Its performance over the past has reflected the bull market in these shares. It was the top performing mutual fund in 1972, 1973, and as of July of 1974 was still going strong. Research Capital Fund is one of the Franklin family, and early in 1974 switched to an all gold portfolio. Franklin Dynatech fund held strong positions in the gold stocks as far back as 1968 in anticipation of the imminent devaluation. Today Research Capital Fund has an advantage over the older International Investors in that they are smaller ($30 million as of October, 1974 compared with I.I.'s $120 million), and thus better able to move in and out of positions in individual stocks, plus they are currently carrying forward certain stock losses from their pre-gold days that will accrue to the advantage of their new shareholders as capital gains are earned on gold shares.

Summary

In summary, gold should be part of every intelligent investor's portfolio. Coins or bullion should be purchased for cash and stored in as risk-free a situation as possible. It would certainly be wise to diversify into both the actual commodity and the gold stocks, as they both have advantages and are a fine complement to each other.

SILVER

While many of the comments relative to gold in the preceding section apply to silver as well, it's necessary for an investor to have a clear understanding that there are substantial differences between the two metals. Silver, like gold, has been esteemed for centuries for both its utility and its beauty. Because of its scarcity, weight, durability, and divisibility, it could serve and has served the function of money in many societies.

Bi-Metallism

C.V. Wright in his booklet "Silver" pointed out that as far back as the Dynasty of Pharaoh Menges (3,500 B.C.) silver was in use as money alongside gold. Its value set by decree, one part of gold was equal to two and one half parts of silver. What value they put on gold in relation to other commodities I don't know, but in all probability the price ratio of silver to gold was the result of the relative abundance of the two metals. Since silver has functioned as a form of money alongside gold in many societies, there have been repeated attempts to enforce a bi-metallic standard. Bi-metallism simply means that both metals are legal currency in a country and, as did Pharaoh Menges, the government establishes the price ratio between them.

In the first coinage act of 1792 the congress of the United States set up two units of value: a gold dollar containing 24.75 grains of pure gold and a silver dollar containing 371.25 grains of pure silver. Since there are 480 grains in an ounce, the "monetary" value of silver was therefore established at $1.2929 per ounce and the "monetary" value of gold was established at $19.3939 per ounce; or a 15-1 ratio between silver and gold.

The impossibility of maintaining this ratio might be better understood if we go back to our simple society and use other barter commodities in place of silver and gold. One unit of the farmer's production equals one unit of the tailor's production equals one unit of the carpenter's production. If the three producers were to decide that this ratio of A equals B equals C must always hold true, then what would happen if the production of one of the three increased (or decreased)? If apples became easier to produce and the farmer had twice as many, yet the value were to remain constant, either he would have more purchasing power than the other producers and could buy up all their production and they would be left with nothing but apples, or they would refuse to sell their

production, prefering to hoard it. In fact, they would all try
to use the abundant commodity to buy up the less abundant
commodities.

The real value of a commodity depends on the quantity
and usefulness of that commodity relative to the quantity
and usefulness of the other commodities in the marketplace.
To say that silver will always bear the same value relationship
to gold is to assume that each will always be constant in
supply and demand. No single commodity is constant in
supply and demand. Thus, when the U.S. instituted a bi-
metallic standard and attempted to legislate a constant ratio,
they were doomed to defeat.

Gresham's Law* went into force. Bad money drives good
money out of circulation. As gold became more plentiful,
people would spend gold dollars and hoard silver dollars; as
silver became more plentiful, people would hoard gold and
spend silver. Even at the time of the original fixing of the
ratio, gold was more valuable than the ratio suggested so it
was hoarded and silver became the nation's circulating
money.

Finally in the 1830's gold was revalued, the ratio was reset
at 16-to-1 and the situation reversed; gold began to circulate
again and silver disappeared. Whenever the free market price
of silver rose above $1.29 per ounce on the open market,
none was offered to the treasury for coinage, and silver coins
quickly disappeared from the market. When it dropped below
$1.29 per ounce, it was sold to the treasury and the dollars
received were then redeemed in gold. Even though it should

---

*Sir Thomas Gresham, founder of the English Royal Exchange, ex-
plained the principal of his law to Queen Elizabeth in 1558. When
two or more kinds of money of equal denomination but different
intrinsic value are in circulation at the same time, the one of highest
intrinsic value will be hoarded and the one of lower intrinsic value
spent. When you find you have a silver quarter and a copper plated
quarter, you'll naturally follow Gresham's Law by keeping the silver
and spending the copper.

have been obvious by this time that bi-mettalism wouldn't work, various forces were lobbying strongly in congress to keep silver on as money.

After the civil war there was a depression during which prices fell to their prewar levels. Those who had contracted debts during the war found it difficult to earn the dollars necessary to repay these debts and pushed for inflationary policies which included expanding the money supply by injecting silver into the currency system at inflated prices. Later on in the century, when the use of silver tapered off in Europe and new mines were opened in the west, the mining interests in the U.S. found the price of silver dropping and pressured congress into passing the Sherman Silver Purchase Act of 1890, which directed the Treasury to buy 4.5 million ounces of silver every month.

All these purchases of silver didn't really save the price of silver, but did result in a drain in the treasury's gold supply and eventually led to the panic of 1893. Faced with declining gold reserves, the government eventually repealed the Sherman Act and also devalued gold slightly (from 24.75 grains to the dollar to 25.8 grains per dollar). Thus, in 1900 the value of gold was set at $20.22 per ounce. Events, including discovery of new gold fields in South Africa, new processes for refining gold from ore, and increasing urban populations, caused increasing prices in general (remember, an increase in the supply of a commodity, in this case gold, causes a decrease in its value relative to other commodities). The increases in prices satisfied the farmers (or "Populists" as they were called) and they stopped pressuring congress to inflate with silver. Silver varied between 65 cents an ounce in 1900 and $1.10 at the peak of the first world war, then drifted downward again. The depression caused the industrial and artistic uses for silver to dry up and by 1932 its free market price hit a low of 29 cents an ounce. At this time the government stepped in again and passed laws to purchase silver.[16]

To understand the government's in-and-out position, it's

necessary to think about their objectives. The Federal bureacracy survives through confiscation of the wealth of the citizens. When the state is able to buy a commodity for one price, monetize it and pass it back to the public at a higher price, it makes a profit. If it can buy silver at 64 cents an ounce, stamp it into silver dollars, and pass those dollars back to the public at $1.29 per ounce, it profits to the extent of 65 cents per ounce. The free market wouldn't pay $1.29 per ounce for silver. It placed a value of about 40 cents per ounce on it. The silver interests were delighted to be able to sell at the higher price to Uncle Sam, and Uncle Sam delighted to pass it on to the gullible public at a price they wouldn't pay for it given free choice. Thus the state could inflate the money supply in a subtle way and keep the difference.

It was politically expeditious during the depression to appear to be creating new jobs and at the same time preventing prices from falling, thus keeping wages and profits up. The method used was to create jobs by creating make-work projects and create the dollars to pay the salaries by inflating the supply of money. Naturally, the state could not get the money to pay these wages from taxing the population, as the people wouldn't have been able or willing to pay the taxes. So the state simply inflated the money supply by whatever means that were convenient. First they had to release the pressure on the gold supplies by severing the dollar ties to gold, which they did by devaluing to $35.00 per ounce from $20.22 per ounce. This effectively increased the gold reserves of the Federal Government by $3 billion. They then sold federal treasury notes, bonds, and bills to the federal reserve bank to the extent allowed by the then existing gold reserve requirements (you see, by devaluing to $35 per ounce they substantially increased their borrowing power). Additionally they manipulated silver to help increase the supply of money. They bought silver at 64 cents per ounce and monetized it by issuing Silver Certificates re-deemable at $1.29 per ounce. A neat trick not at all understood by the public.

From that time on, and no doubt to the disappointment of the politicians, silver began to become more valuable. The second world war created a great demand for the metal, and after the war the boom in electronics and photography caused industrial consumption to rise dramatically. The free market price of silver then began to climb toward the official government price of $1.2929 and as it rose, it became less and less profitable for the state to buy the metal and mint it into coins. Soon silver coins began to disappear from circulation, and the government's silver supply began to dwindle as new coins were minted, placed into circulation, and in turn hoarded.

Silver users preferred to purchase foreign silver to domestic silver up until 1955, because before that time the Treasury support price was higher than the market price, thus domestic suppliers could sell to the treasury at a greater price than users were paying for foreign silver. The treasury stocks increased by the amount of the purchases and decreased by the coinage. As far as the money supply was concerned, however, it was increased by the silver whether held in stockpile or issued in coinage.

After 1955, and until 1961, the market price approximated the treasury support price and the trend reversed. It was as cheap to buy from domestic sources as from foreign sources so users purchased from three sources; the treasury, domestic producers and foreign producers. From 1961 on, the treasury supply began to dwindle rapidly because of new coinage and user purchases. The treasury free silver stockpile reached its peak of 222 million ounces in 1959 (that was in addition to 1,700 million ounces used as backing for silver certificates). By 1960 the supply of free silver was down to 22 million ounces and the legislature was now ready to release the 1,700 million ounces.

The tables had completely turned. What originally was a bonanza to an inflation hungry bureacracy now became a millstone. While originally they were able to inflate the money supply by buying silver cheaply and monetizing it,

now that the price had risen they not only could not
continue to reap the benefits of the price differential, the
very fact that they were bound to back the silver certificate
and to mint silver coins prevented them from further
inflation. Therefore, it was necessary to get rid of silver as a
monetary metal completely. President Kennedy was in office
when the crisis point was reached in 1961 and he made the
decision to demonetize silver. But he really didn't have a
choice, faced with the need of the state to increase the
money supply in order to survive. Nor did Johnson have a
choice when he made the decision in 1964 to stop minting
silver coins. These were inevitable consequences of an
inflating money supply and the need to be free of restrictions
on that inflation. At this point in time the price of silver has
been fluctuating between $3.50 and $7.00 per ounce.

The Future

The ultimate factor that will determine the future price
will be supply and demand. The federal state is now out of
the silver market almost completely. They still maintain a
strategic stockpile which they could dump on the market at
some future date, but since it is estimated at less than 200
million ounces it shouldn't have a prolonged effect. Of course
they could step in at any time and confiscate silver, or fix the
price by selling or buying at some set price. The question is,
why would they? They did it in 1934 because they wanted to
inflate the money supply. But once the inflationary mechanism in any country has reached the state it has in this
country, where we have demonetized *all* metals and inflation
is accomplished merely by monetizing debt instead of
production, there is no real reason to interfere with the
pricing of individual commodities.* The objectives of the

---

*This statement should be modified to take into consideration wage
and price controls used to make a show of fighting inflation or used to
expand the power of the bureaucracy.

state are to support its own survival and expansion by any means possible, and since this can't be done through taxation alone, the state will have to continue to do it through inflation. Since the monetary metals are roadblocks to real inflation, they'll have to be demonetized.

Formerly when a country wished to prevent the ownership of gold and silver during inflationary periods, it was to prevent the citizens from using these metals as mediums of exchange. Now, with no countries any longer on a gold or silver standard, a state doesn't have to worry that its citizens will begin using the gold backed currency of another country for external trading, and its also unlikely that people will revert to the inconvenience of the barter system, whether the medium they're using to barter with is gold, silver, or potatoes. The power of most countries to fix wages and prices in terms of their own legal tender currency is also a deterrant to the bypassing of that currency by the population. The Federal Reserve Bank controls the currency inflation in this country, and even if an individual wanted to operate on a barger basis and bypass the legal tender currency, he would be able to do this only on a small scale since we are a nation that operates more and more on credit, that credit coming from bank borrowing.

Let's make the assumption that in the future the government will step out of the role of price controller of the monetary metals. These metals will be demonetized by all major nations, and prices will be functions solely of supply and demand. Demand will come from: 1. industrial users, 2. Hoarders, 3. Speculators. Speculators can be more or less discounted over the long term as they don't consume, but merely buy from the market and resell to the market. Industrial use can be predicted over the short term, but may be unpredictable over the longer term. For example, substitutes can be developed for any material for almost any application given proper technological development. Uses as a store-of-value will depend on the need to place assets in secure positions. As economic conditions in the world become more precarious and as central banks continue to inflate their currencies, people everywhere will turn more and more to store-of-value assets and less and less toward business investments. This will create a greater demand for gold and silver and they should rise in price.

All things being taken into consideration (current supply, industrial demand, etc.), is the market price of silver realistic or has it been driven artifically high by speculators? Assuming you answer that question, will industrial demand increase or decrease, and will supplies increase or decrease? We know for certain that if supply-demand forces were constant in the future, then the price of the metal would increase at whatever rate the money supply increased. If we are experiencing 15% per year inflation, the price of the commodity would go up that amount. Figure 11 shows the production and consumption of silver over the past 30 years. The future deficit should be covered by an increasing price of silver, and in addition, any further inflation of the money supply should carry the price up even higher.

Summary

In summary, silver still looks like a good long term store-of-value asset. Unless you're a speculator, however, stay away from buying on margin. Buy for cash, take delivery, and store it in a safe place. Don't be rattled by price fluctuations. The silver market is volatile because it's currently controlled by speculators; it will be fluctuating wildly over the next few years. Remember that the long term view bodes for increasing inflation and store-of-value commodities will increase in price.

OTHER STORE—OF—VALUE ASSETS

Storing your excess production for consumption at a later time is the name of the game. As we have seen, gold and

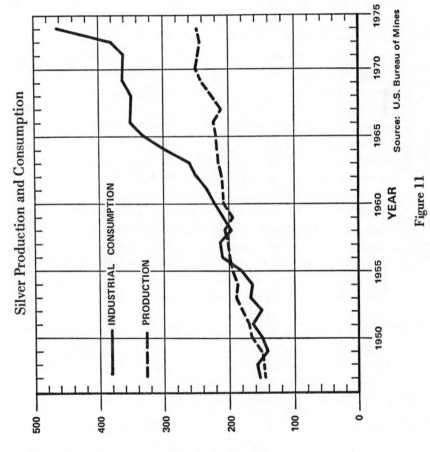

Silver Production and Consumption

INDUSTRIAL CONSUMPTION

PRODUCTION

MILLIONS OF OUNCES

YEAR

Source: U.S. Bureau of Mines

Figure 11

silver have the characteristics of sound money and are
eminently storable. How about other commodities, manufactured and otherwise? How about saving the commodities
that you'll be consuming?

In the case of food, it's perishable. A person can store
away a quantity of certain kinds of dried or canned food,
and over a reasonably short length of time expect to be
able to consume it. But how about long periods of time,
like ten years? Most of the food value, or at least the appeal,
regardless of the method used for preserving, will have been
leached away. Long term storage of food under present technology is just not too practical. This should not deter you from
purchasing the maximum amount you can conveniently
store and consume over short periods. I certainly recommend
keeping a full larder. A year's supply of all staple products
used around the home will mean fewer trips to the store and
a substantial savings as inflation rolls along.

Other things that might eventually be consumed are energy
products (oil, coal, etc.), housing, clothing, means of transportation, and appliances. Most manufactured articles suffer
from two kinds of loss; functional obsolescence, and physical deterioration. Thus an automobile purchased in 1956 and
stored for use in 1976 would lose value due to deterioration
of certain of its parts, whether it was used or not, and additionally would lose value due to design improvements on
newer models. Another drawback to advance purchasing is
the cost of storage. A lifetime supply of automobiles would
take a significant amount of storage space; hardly practical.

When we look for commodities to use to store value, we
look for the following attributes:

1. Durability (no functional or physical
obsolescence).
2. Limited supply.
3. Consistent demand (regardless of world economic
situation).

4. Ease of storage.
5. Protectable against individual or government theft.

In light of these criteria it's easy to see why gold and silver have become standards of wealth and obvious store-of-value mechanisms.

Metals

Other metals can perform the same function, but in other metals we are looking at different characteristics. For one thing, few metals are really valued because of their beauty. For the most part other metals are industrial commodities, and the demand for them depends on the level of industrial production. The higher the cost-per-pound of a metal, the more practical it is as a store-of-value asset, providing other points are consistent. Platinum, for example, is more expensive than gold due to its rarity. Furthermore, it is unlikely that any substitute will be found that will cause demand for the metal to fall off. Industrially, it is used alone, or alloyed with other metals, as a catalyst in the manufacture of acids, in electrical contacts and laboratory ware. Its properties and abundance make it cheaper than its next substitute.

From a storage standpoint platinum would be the metal most likely to serve the purpose of storing wealth. It can be purchased in ingot form in weights from one ounce up.

Copper is relatively plentiful in the earth and its properties of conductivity, strength and malleability make it particularly useful in wire, sheets, and bars that need to conduct electricity. When alloyed with zinc or tin it becomes brass or bronze and is extremely resistant to corrosion.

Supplies will fluctuate somewhat due to potential new discoveries of the metal, as well as recovery from scrap, while demand is unlikely to taper off. As a store-of-value it would be fine, except that it's bulky, and any significant amount of

it could present storage problems. Some people have begun
to save copper pennies, thinking they'll increase in value as
copper moves up in price. There will be a penny's worth of
copper in a penny when the price of copper reaches $1.37
per pound, and certainly copper could reach that in the near
future. Still, the effort to collect and count a significant
amount of pennies would probably eliminate the profits of
hoarding them.

Raw Commodities Via the Futures Market

There are certain other usable commodities that could be
held and should retain their value. Included would be sugar,
wheat, corn, soybeans, iron, manganese, zinc, lumber, wool,
cotton, hides, etc. For most of these commodities the
significant problems would be storage, spoilage and remar-
keting at the point of sale. It is possible to buy these
commodities without having to worry about either storage or
spoilage, and that is through the futures market.

The commodities furtures market is considered to be a
tool either of the manufacturer and raw commodity producer, or of the speculator. Originally it was set up as a way
for the producer and manufacturer to hedge their risks of
price fluctuations. For example, when a manufacturer of
breakfast cereals knows he needs 40,000 bushels of wheat
out of the fall harvest, but doesn't know whether that harvest
would be good or bad, or what that wheat might cost him
when he finally buys it, he may go to the farmer and contract
for future delivery at a specified price. He is now able to
accurately predict his costs and maintain a more stable
business. The farmer is protected in this way also, for if the

price of wheat is down in the fall due to bumper crops, then he still has sold a portion of his crop at the contract price. If the crop is poor and the price of wheat is up, then he loses the benefit of the higher price.

Speculators get into the market in order to profit from the price fluctuations in these commodities. If they feel that the crop is going to be good, and the price of the commodity will come down at harvest, they can act as the producer, selling a crop now at a higher price than they think it will bring at harvest and then when delivery time comes they can go to the farmer and buy the goods they need to fulfill their contract. By selling now at a high price, and buying back at a lower price in the future, they could profit from the difference. Likewise if they think the crop will be bad, they could buy from the producer now at a low price, and sell to the manufacturer at a higher price when the commodity is to be delivered.

The commodity futures market operates through a group of "exchanges" in various cities throughout the United States. Leading grain futures exchanges are in Chicago, Minneapolis and Kansas City. Cotton and wood exchanges are in New York, as are those for sugar, cocoa, potatoes and metals. Individuals and organizations dealing in one way or another in these commodities become members of the exchange and can then trade on the exchange. Non-members trade through brokerage houses whose partners are members.

Commodities are traded on these exchanges in "contracts." A contract for each commodity will be standard for that commodity and will specify the amount of the commodity, the grade, and the time of delivery. When you buy silver, for example, you will buy a contract for delivery in a specific month and it will be for 10,000 ounces of .999 fine silver. Each commodity has a fixed commission and quantity. Figure 12 lists ten of the more common commodities and their contract size and commissions.[17]

Commodity	Contract	Commission
Cocoa	30,000 lbs.	$60.00
Coffee	37,500 lbs.	$60.00 to $70.00
Copper	25,000 lbs.	$36.00
Cotton	50,000 lbs.	$45.00 when price is under 40 cents. Add $5.00 for every 5 cent rise thereafter.
Wheat, Corn, Oats, Soybeans (Chicago)	5,000 Bushels	$25.00 (oats) $30.00 (others)
Lumber	100,000 Bd. Ft.	$40.00
Platinum	50 ounces	$45.00 + $2.00 Clearance Fee
Silver	10,000 ounces	$45.00 + 50 cent Exchange Fee
Sugar #10 (Raw Domestic)	50 tons (112,000 lbs.)	$42.00

Figure 12

Normally buying a contract for future delivery of a commodity is handled by going to your local brokerage house, telling the broker what you want, and putting down a deposit on the contract. The swinging reputation enjoyed by those who speculate in commodities comes from the fact that the amount of deposit in relation to the full price of the contract is relatively small, being usually 10% to 20% of the total. Thus if silver were selling at $4.00 per ounce for delivery in July, a 10,000 ounce contract would cost $40,000. The buyer would simply put down a deposit of $4,000 and pay the balance when the contract was to be delivered. Of course most people don't want to take delivery of the physical commodity, but sell their contract sometime before the delivery date. If the price of silver began to move down during the time the contract was being held, the value of the contract might fall below $36,000, at which time the equity represented by the $4,000 deposit would be lost. In other words, if silver in this instance dropped from $4.00 per ounce to $3.60 per ounce the buyer would be wiped out. Sometime before that happens the contract owner must put up more deposit money or lose the contract. Since commodities are prone to wide price fluctuations, speculators in the commodities futures market can become rich or poor very rapidly.

Speculating with small down payments is only one way to play the commodities market, however. If you are sincerely concerned about inflation and would like to hold certain commodities as a hedge against the loss of purchasing power of the dollar, then it is possible to buy a commodities contract for cash. In fact, even better than buying for cash, you could, in the case of the silver contract above mentioned, take the $40,000 purchase price, put $4,000 down on the silver, and put the other $36,000 in treasury bills. Since the commodities contract calls for no interest, you will essentially own the commodity, pay no storage charges, and be earning interest on the money at the same time. Buying the commodity in this fashion has one other advantage; you don't have to worry about storage or handling (as long as you don't take delivery at the expiration of the contract). Also, you'll find that commission charges on purchase of a commodity might be lower through the futures market than they are when buying the actual goods.

To use the commodities futures market as a hedge against inflation you'll have to select a number of representative commodities that you feel will rise in price along with inflation. You'll buy a contract in the commodity, and sell that contract just before it expires. Then you'll repurchase another contract for future delivery. Of course, at the point that the futures market begins to correctly anticipate the inflation factor in its prices, this strategy will no longer work,

for the future price at which you'll be buying will already
have inflation built in and there will be no profit to you. For
example, when silver is selling today at $4.00 per ounce and
the price for delivery a year from today is $6.00 per ounce,
even if silver does rise 15% from today's price, you'll only get
your money back out and no profit. The investor who wants
to profit from inflation will study the current commodities
prices and find commodities in which the future price has not
increased, thereby allowing him to wager on an inflationary
rise.

Raw Land

Another commodity that you can purchase in order to
store value is raw land. It is in limited supply, constant
demand, provides its own storage, and is reasonably durable
(assuming you're not too close to the edge of a cliff or
meandering river). Increasing population makes it seem
scarcer. Its value is more difficult to determine accurately
than the values of the precious metals, for its quality is
inconsistent. The variables of location, soil, population
movement, and the lack of a wide auction market mean that
a buyer can easily pay more than the land could be resold
for, while in constrast gold is quoted daily on worldwide
markets. Any novice can buy gold or silver and by checking a
variety of sources be assured of a price reasonably close to
the general market price, while buying raw land at the right
price is really a job for a good negotiator who's knowledgeable about local real estate conditions.

The greatest disadvantage of land is that its ownership is a
matter of public record, and its use is subject to the whim of
the government. Zoning laws can restrict its use, environ-
mental agencies can prevent its use, and the government can
demand easements or simply confiscate it under the laws of
eminent domain. It's impossible to hide it from the prying
eyes of the tax collector, and confiscatory taxation by the
state is an ever present threat, especially when the state is in
economic trouble.

If you plan to use raw land as an investment vehicle, here are a few suggestions. Don't buy land from subdividers. Land deals like Rancho California, Salton Sea, California City, etc. are designed for the unsophisticated and sold on pure emotion, and usually result in profits only for the developer. They are generally large parcels of land in areas too far out to have current value, divided up into small parcels of land and sold a few dollars down and a few dollars a month. Most if not all the money you pay down goes into the salesman's pocket, and the syndicator gets his profit from the interest and principal payments you'll make. It's unusual for the syndicator not to have his investment back from your first few payments, even though you may be stuck with a ten year contract. If your land is fifty miles beyond the outback, and you're told that prices should double within a couple of years, make an estimate of the amount of land still in the syndicator's inventory that he'll be selling to next year's customers. Then figure out how likely he'll be to buy your land back at a higher price when he still has more land to sell. Also figure out why a buyer might want your lot when they can buy a new lot at half the price from the syndicator.

If you've decided to buy raw land, buy it from a private party and be prepared to put some time and effort into its selection. Spend a lot of time checking comparable sales in the area, buy in a semi-developed area, and don't buy on margin unless you plan to use the asset as a speculation.

One possibility that shouldn't be overlooked is the operation of some type of business on the raw land while you're holding it. The land becomes the store of value and the business generates enough income to pay the taxes and hopefully a profit as well. Examples would be the operation of a mobile home park or a travel trailer park on a piece of suburban land. The improvements should be minimal in cost in relation to the value of the property and could be amortized over the holding period.

I'm not going to attempt to give you the information

necessary to make you successful at buying raw land or most of the other vehicles mentioned in this book. The purpose here is to acquaint you with the characteristics of each of the assets, and what the relative risks and advantages are to each. In other words, to help you organize and categorize, and to make comprehensible the myriad of offerings available.

Art

Certain other commodities are always mentioned when it comes to store of value. Artists and art dealers have played very heavily on the idea that art is a great hedge against inflation, and should be part of everyone's portfolio. It's true that works of fine art, done by artists of widely established reputation, have appreciated dramatically in value during periods of inflation. Unfortunately most of the dramatic price rises that you hear about are for great works by world renowned and usually dead artists. These works are passing through the hands of extremely knowledgeable and dedicated art connoisseurs. The unknowledgeable investor will be buying less well-known works by less well-known artists, and will be paying retail prices through art galleries. Since most galleries are working on a markup of 40%, you'll have to have a 40% appreciation in the work in order to have a gallery interested in buying it back at what you paid for it.

The idea that the average person can select art works of new and promising artists, buy them and hold them for long term appreciation is lunacy. There is no doubt that a few of the unknown artists who are today toiling behind hot paint brushes in dimlit garages around the world will someday be discovered, and their early works will command prices hundreds of times what they sell for today. The sheer quantity of new art being produced makes finding the budding Picasso a task far more difficult than finding the proverbial needle in the haystack. Even the super-pros of the art world, those prestigious dealers who comb the art fairs, galleries and studios around the world, who have thousands of sources constantly supplying them with examples of fresh new talent, and who really know talent when they see it, even they are rarely lucky enough to come across the diamond in the raw. Your chances of buying a work from an artist at the Laguna Art Festival, or any of the thousands of galleries in New York, Chicago, or Los Angeles, and having it ever appreciate enough to be worth what you paid for it are about zero. It can be done. But it's just about as reasonable an ambition as hitting five sevens in a row on the crap table at Las Vegas.

If you want to make money at new art, become a dealer. Don't become a collector. If you want to become a collector, do it for the sheer pleasure of the art itself, not for the money.

For those with enough money and a taste for collecting established master works the risks and rewards are slightly different. Inflation will certainly carry the value of the works up. You must still be cognizant of your potential market for resale, however. Selling back to the galleries will mean that you'll need to have the work appreciate at least high enough that they can make their normal profit by buying back from you and reselling. Otherwise you'll have to find a buyer outside the galleries, and that is almost unheard of. Any product is worth only as much as another person is willing to pay for it, and it stands to reason that it's going to cost money to find that buyer who's willing to pay.

You should also recall that inflation is not the only risk to one's capital. Depression is also a risk. What would happen to art in a depression? It's almost certain that the market would diminish considerably. When there isn't a lot of money floating around, all of the "luxury" industries fall off, and art is certainly a luxury industry.

Gems

So much for art; how about diamonds? Diamonds are similar in nature to gold and silver, in that they are natural elements that have both beauty and utility. Unlike gold and silver, however, they are not uniform in quality, not divisible into equally valuable parts, and not readily identifiable by amateurs. They certainly can fill the role of store-of-value assets and do for many wealthy people. For the average investor, however, there are too many problems associated with purchase and ownership of gems to make them attractive.

1. Selection. How do you determine that the price you're paying is the correct price for the stone? It must be appraised, and given the variation in opinion of appraisers, how can you ever take their word for it that a given stone has a given value? Especially when the appraisal probably came from the person selling the stone.

2. Mark-up. How can you hope to make money on a product when the dealer markup can be as high as 100%? Buying diamonds from a retail jeweler will put you at a starting point at least 50% behind breakeven. A pretty poor store-of-value.

3. Resale. Ever tried to resell a diamond? Ads in the paper can bring in all sorts of unsavory inquiries. Better keep the diamonds in a safe-deposit box and take the would-be purchaser there for the examination and transaction. Even then, keep a close eye on his hands. How about selling them back to the diamond merchant. He was all friendly when you wanted to buy. Now, he's totally disinterested. After all, he can buy the same thing wholesale that you want to sell him at retail. He may buy it, but you may not like the price.

In short, gems are great if you're an expert and have wholesale sources. They should hold up well in any inflationary situation and as they are really a form of hard money won't fare terribly badly during a depression. Of course the value of gems would fall if the jewelry industry sales drop during times of low employment, but the long range price should be all right. They're just not a sensible investment for the average person.

Summary

The above is only a partial list of store-of-value assets. The important thing to realize is that in these tumultuous times you must hold a significant percentage of your wealth in the form of real, intrinsically valuable commodities. They present as safe a haven as is possible against the risk of inflation, and offer protection against most other risks as well. The type you choose will depend on your facilities for storage, your available capital, and your areas of expertise. So learn to recognize a store-of-value asset when you see it, and stock up while there's still time.

LENDING

The single most popular form of putting money to work is by lending it out. As of March, 1974, individuals, partnerships, and corporations had loaned the following sums to institutions in the U.S.[18]

Commercial Banks	$378,000,000,000
Life Insurance Companies...	255,000,000,000
Mutual Savings Banks	108,000,000,000
Savings & Loan Companies ..	235,000,000,000
Total	$976,000,000,000

That figure doesn't include corporate and government bonds. What's remarkable about this amount is that the people who have placed these funds in the loan market have done so because they want security and income. But let's take a close look at the facts.

You remember in Chapter II we discussed the concept of True Rate of Return. The net return you receive for the use of your capital is the advertised or apparent rate of return less the taxes and less the loss in purchasing power caused by rising prices. In some cases it's possible to postpone or eliminate state and federal taxes, but once money is loaned out and the contract calls for repayment to the lender in legal tender currency, there is no way to overcome erosion of purchasing power due to inflation. Figure 13 lists the more common types of loans that you can make, their apparent rate of return (which will vary of course), and a hypothetical loss due to taxes. Although the tax loss is estimated at 50% of the income received, your actual loss will depend on your tax bracket. Column 6 of the chart assumes that the income from the investment is funneled into a tax deferred or tax free trust, and thus is the apparent rate of return less only the rate of inflation.

The rate of inflation is given at 12% per year. This is quite an arbitrary figure. In 1973 the government said the consumer price index rose 8.2%. Through July of 1974 the consumer price index was moving forward at an annual rate of almost 12% and threatening to move higher. But even at that, assume at this point in time that the rate of inflation could be held to only 12% and that it might remain at that level. If there is no taxation on your return, then you must get at least 12% (or whatever the rate of inflation is) in order to break even. Looking at the chart, how much of the above mentioned $976 billion now invested in loans is earning a positive rate of return for its owners? Better yet, ask yourself this question: How much of *your* money is loaned out right now and how much of it is breaking even in purchasing power?* Let's look more closely at some of the common vehicles for lending money.

_____

*You should not necessarily figure that just because you have your money in a tax-deferred trust, like a corporate pension or profit sharing plan, that you can completely discount taxes. When that money comes out it will be taxable, and who knows what the rates will be then?

TRUE RATE OF RETURN ON LOANS					
LOAN	APPARENT RATE OF RETURN	INFLATION	TAXES	TRUE RATE OF RETURN	TRUE RATE OF RETURN IN TRUST
Cash Value Life Insurance	3%	12%	-0-	(9%)	(9%)
Bank, Checking	0%	12%	-0-	(12%)	(12%)
Bank, Savings	6%	12%	3%	(9%)	(6%)
Savings & Loan	7%	12%	3.5%	(8.5%)	(5%)
Municipal Bonds	6%	12%	-0-	(6%)	(6%)
Corporate Bonds	10%	12%	5%	(7%)	(2%)
1st Trust Deeds	9%	12%	4.5%	(7.5%)	(3%)
2nd Trust Deeds	12%	12%	6%	(6%)	-0-
Treasury Bills	9%	12%	4.5%	(7.5%)	(3%)
Annuities	4.5%	12%	2.25%	(9.75%)	N.A.
Floating Rate Securities	11%	12%	5.5%	(6.5%)	(1%)

Figure 13

LIFE INSURANCE COMPANIES

Life insurance companies borrow money from policy holders in a variety of ways. First they sell cash value life insurance. That means you're buying a term insurance policy with a mandatory savings account attached (see Chapter IV for a more detailed explanation). The insurance company will pay you somewhere between 2% and 4% interest on that account, and the tax on the income will be deferred until the cash value is withdrawn from the policy. Even without considering tax, your net loss on capital is somewhere between 8% and 10% per year at a 12% inflation rate! The life insurance company also will ask you to leave your dividends with them to accumulate at interest. Here they'll pay 4% to 5% and again your loss, not considering taxes, is 7% to 8% per year. In this case, however, the interest is taxable as accrued, which could bring your loss up to 9% to 10% annually. Life insurance companies also ask that the death proceeds of a policy be left with them and they'll pay the widow or other beneficiary a monthly income, that income being a fixed rate of interest plus a portion of the capital. The rate usually is 4% to 5%, again a serious loss to you.

BANKS

Banks pay a variety of interest rates depending on federal and state laws. On checking accounts they pay nothing, so any currency you leave in that account will cost you the entire rate of inflation. Passbook savings accounts typically pay from 5% to 6%. Assuming this interest is fully taxable, you're losing 8% per year or more, depending on your tax bracket and the real rate of inflation. In the more lucrative time certificates of deposit, if you deposit a minimum amount of money and guarantee to leave it with the bank for longer periods of time, (6 months, 1 year, 5 years, etc.) you might currently get rates as high as 12%. But even then,

deducting the taxes and the loss of purchasing power, you'll
still find yourself losing up to 6% per year. One sidelight
about bank interest rates. Banks don't depend on the level of
interest rates in order to make a profit, for their profit comes
from the spread between what they have to pay for money
and what they can lend it out for. If they must pay 5% to
attract money, they can lend it out for 10% and profit by the
difference. As the rate of inflation continues to climb, bank
interest rates will get higher and higher, simply because they
must pay enough interest to attract depositors and depositors
won't be willing to leave money on deposit at a rate of return
lower than the rate of inflation. At least not for long.

An example of this is seen in Brazil. In an interesting
article in *The Journal of Money Credit and Banking*, Mr.
Antonio M. Silviera pointed out that Brazil has had an
average rate of inflation of over 30% per year for over 20
years![19] Interest rates likewise kept pace with inflation,
climbing to an astronomical 35% per year. Interestingly,
Brazil has usury laws as we have in the U.S., but they are
easily circumvented:

> "The explanation for the extremely low level of
> the stated prime rate in Brazil lies in two laws, the
> usury law and the gold clause law, both promulgated
> in 1933. The usury law fixed an upper bound of 12
> percent per year on all interest rates. And the gold
> clause law "forbade contractual payments except in
> domestic currency at its legal value," i.e., monetary
> correction was outlawed. But the banks were able to
> circumvent the ceiling to a large extent. This was
> done mainly by charging a "service fee," a rate which
> in no way differs from the interest rate."

You can't expect to be able to borrow money in an
inflating economy at less than the rate of inflation unless
you're borrowing from unsophisticated lenders, and lenders
tend to gain sophistication as time goes on. The banks,
savings and loans and life insurance industries are borrowing
now at ridiculous rates from a public unfamiliar with

hyperinflation. This can't last. As you watch the interest rates go up at your neighborhood bank, don't be misled into thinking you're profiting because of the high rates. They're going up because the rate of inflation is going up, and you're in no more of a position to profit than you were when the rates were 2% or 3% per year.

SAVINGS & LOANS

The $235 billion in Savings and Loan companies (formerly called "Building and Loans") indicates a strong trust in these institutions. Most people, however, don't understand how they work and how they make a profit, let alone what risks are involved in depositing money with them. Unlike banks they are unable to leverage their deposits. If you deposit $10,000 in a savings and loan, that money will be loaned out on a long-term mortgage. They'll pay you about 6% to 8% on your money while it's on deposit and will try to earn 12% or more on that money by lending it to property owners.* Laws vary from state to state, but generally Savings and Loans must keep at least 5% of their net assets in liquid securities such as government bonds. The other 95% can be loaned out on mortgages. In their advertising on radio and television, they mention only their assets when talking of the safety and strength of their organization. "Four billion dollars strong" sounds mighty reassuring, until you find out that their liabilities are $4 billion also. Since almost all the money you deposit with them is loaned out on real estate mortgages, their position in the event of a serious recession is tenuous. If an economic collapse occurs, you'd better get to your local Savings and Loan before that 5% liquid capital is used up. In the event of a serious collapse it is likely many people will be unable to continue making mortgage payments. During the

---

*While the mortgage rate on a piece of real estate may only be 9% the loan points, fees and prepayment penalties bring up the net take substantially.

great depression thousands of Building and Loan companies closed their doors and depositors' losses amounted to hundreds of millions of dollars.

Even without considering the risks involved in the event of a depression, how about the rate of return on your capital? The chart shows that if you're in a high tax bracket, your net annual *loss* on your capital will be about 8% at a 12% inflation rate. Not so good, everything considered.

U.S. GOVERNMENT SECURITIES

The United States Government and its various agencies issue a number of different types of securities. These fall under the category of bonds although they are called by a variety of names. They include U.S. Treasury Bills, Notes, Bonds, and Certificates and Securities issued by instrumentalities of the U.S. Government such as Fanny Mae (Federal National Mortgage Association), Genny Mae, (Government National Mortgage Association), FHDA (Farmers Home Administration), The Federal Land Bank and Federal Home Loan Bank. These instrumentalities issue notes or debentures, or guarantee them for other issuers. The difference between these securities is primarily one of yield and duration.

If the choice is between a Savings and Loan account at 6% and a treasury bill at 9%, then certainly the T-bill is the better buy. It's far more secure and a 50% better return. But it's still not good enough in hyper-inflation. While the principle is secure, how can you afford the loss in purchasing power?

BONDS

When a corporation wants to borrow money it issues corporate bonds. These are simply promises to repay a given amount of money at a given time in the future, and to pay interest at a specified rate until the bond is redeemed.

The price or value of a bond is a function of the strength
of the issuing company and the general level of interest rates.
For example, a company sells you a $1,000 bond maturing in
20 years at a time when the general interest rate for that
particular quality of bond is 8%. As interest rates rise a
person looking for interest bearing securities would have a
choice between a new bond issue yielding say 10%, and
buying your bond from you which is only yielding 8%. In
order to induce him to buy your bond you'll have to offer it
to him at a discount, and that discount will be calculated to
make his investment yield him the 10% rate that the market
is offering. Your bond might offer a couple of pluses
however, one being that it is "seasoned," or has established a
history of prompt payment of interest, and secondly by
buying at a discount, that is by paying only $800 for your
bond, he is assured of a capital gain of $200 when the bond is
redeemed at maturity. Usually the tax benefit of this
potential capital gain is calculated into the discount on the
bond and his current yield will be something less than the
10% that might be available on a new issue.

As far as risk of loss of the principal, it is unlikely that a
well selected bond portfolio will suffer substantial losses due
to the bankruptcy of the issuing companies. Companies do go
bankrupt, of course, but even then the bondholders are first
in line after the creditors and before the stockholders to
benefit from the liquidation of the assets. A wide diversification and prudent selection of risks would make chances of
loss of capital negligible. The real problems will come with
runaway inflation, for history reveals that in the past
bondholders have suffered the same fate as all holders of debt
instruments; total loss of purchasing power of the principal.
Even if we don't slide into runaway inflation the loss on 8%
or 10% yields, especially if the yield is taxable, is enough to
be significant. It takes the investment out of the category of
"sound" or "prudent" and guarantees that if you keep it long
enough, you'll be a sure loser.

Municipal Bonds

Municipal bonds differ only slightly from corporate or federal bonds. They are issued by states and municipalities and are backed either by the taxing authority of the municipality (general obligation bonds) or by the revenue from some project like a turnpike (revenue bonds). The single characteristic that differentiates them from other bonds is that the income is free of federal and sometimes state income tax. This means that the true rate of return is proportionately higher than a corporate or federal bond would be. One of the more misleading advertisements regarding tax-free municipal bonds has to do with the rate of return realized by a high-tax-bracket investor. Sales organizations working with municipal bonds will frequently produce tables showing that if you're in a 70% tax bracket the yield of a 5% municipal bond is the equivalent of a 16.7% yield if that yield were taxable. Unfortunately you'll have a hard time compounding your money at 16.7% with these bonds even if you're in that tax bracket. The compounding will still take place at 5% (or whatever the bond is yielding), and the True Rate of Return will still be calculated by subtracting the current rate of inflation from the Apparent Rate of Return. Municipal bonds generally have lower yields than corporate bonds of an equivalent quality, because the market is willing to pay more for them due to their tax-free qualities.

One further caution, although this might seem obvious to some. Never put municipal bonds into a tax-deferred pension, profit-sharing, or Keogh Plan. If you did, the yield would eventually become taxable, as all gains in these plans are taxed on distribution. If you want bonds in a plan, buy the higher yielding corporate or federal securities.

Bond Funds

One vehicle for buying bonds is the bond fund. These are professionally managed portfolios of bonds, and they can be either open-end or closed-end type mutual funds. The advantages of buying bonds through these funds is as follows:

1. *A broader diversification of bonds can be purchased with a small amount of money.* The bond portfolio of the fund may contain two or three hundred different issues and each shareholder owns a proportionate share of each bond.

2. *There is no coupon clipping to do.* Managers of the fund take care of clipping the coupons and mailing away for the interest on each bond as the interest becomes due. Then they mail one monthly or quarterly check to each shareholder.

3. *You can conveniently reinvest the interest* you receive on your bonds in more shares of the bond fund, thus making the compounding of that interest simpler. It is difficult to take small interest checks from your individual bonds and buy more bonds.

4. *You don't have to worry about the custody of the bonds themselves.*

The disadvantage of the bond funds is that they charge a management fee (and in some cases an entrance fee) that you wouldn't pay if you were buying individual issues.

Examples of bond funds currently being offered are:

Westminster Bond Fund: A fund managed by the Wellington management company, an old line mutual fund management company headquartered in Valley Forge, Pa. It invests in general investment grade corporate bonds rated in the top four grades, but can put up to 30% of the portfolio into lower grade bonds, convertible securities, or preferred stocks. This is an open-end bond fund, meaning that they can continually sell more shares of the fund, and that they must redeem your shares when offered at net asset value.

Keystone Bond Funds: Keystone is one of the oldest mutual fund organizations in the U.S. Keystone Company of Boston operates three different open-end bond funds, offer-

ing a range of yields. B-1 offers the lowest yield and the
highest security, while B-4 offers the highest yield and the
lowest security. You can transfer from one bond fund to
another, or from a bond fund into one of Keystone's
common stock funds, but there is a charge for such a
transfer.

Capital Preservation Fund: A fund which invests primarily
in U.S. Government securities, and certificates of deposit,
Capital Preservation Fund offers a high current yield (assuming that current government yields are high), the ultimate in
safety, and a high degree of liquidity. This is a no-load fund
which will redeem shares without penalty no matter how long
held, so that a person with funds to invest on a short term
could still obtain the maximum yield.

Nuveen Fund: This is a closed-end fund that buys only
tax-exempt municipal bonds. They have a continuing series
of offerings and the series you buy into will determine your
yield. After each offering is completed they take the money
invested and buy a portfolio of bonds. The income from the
bonds is distributed quarterly or monthly and the bonds are
held in the portfolio until they mature. As each bond
matures and is redeemed the money is distributed to the fund
shareholders. One disadvantage to this type of fund is that
they hold offerings from various states so that your income
will never be exempt from state income tax. If you buy
individual bonds you can select those from within your local
state and thus be exempt from state income tax as well as
federal. Nuveen's load for buying is 4.5%, and their annual
management fee and expenses run about .1%.

MORTGAGES AND TRUST DEEDS

Another method of lending out money at a high rate of
return is by lending it to an individual or a company, and
taking in return the deed to a piece of property as collateral
for the loan. Since the deed is held in trust until the loan is

repaid, it is said to be a trust deed. When an owner has borrowed against the property and signed over a first deed of trust, he may borrow again and issue a second deed of trust. The second trust deed is more risky and generally offers a higher yield in return for the increased risk. A trust deed can be sold at a discount by a holder who wishes to get rid of it rather than hold it to maturity. A buyer could thus get a higher yield by paying less than the face value of the trust deed. Mortgages or trust deeds are favorite investments of life insurance companies, as well as savings and loans. Inasmuch as these institutions collect points, prepayment penalties, and other fees, the effective rate of interest is higher than the rate indicated on the note.

Real Estate Investment Trusts

An individual interested in lending money with property as collateral has the choice of buying trust deeds individually or investing in a pooling fund of trust deeds. These go under the name of mortgage Real Estate Investment Trusts (REITs), a relatively new vehicle whose assets have grown to about $20 billion from only $1 billion in the past five years.

There are two types of Real Estate Investment Trusts; equity and mortgage. Equity REITs invest directly in the ownership of real estate, while the mortgage REITs invest in mortgages on real estate. Typically the REIT will raise public funds, then borrow from commercial lending sources as heavily as possible and invest the entire amount in mortgages. The spread between the cost of the money they borrow and the return they receive from the higher yielding mortgages is added to the profit of the shareholders. Assuming this yield rises above what the market in general is paying for borrowed funds, the value of the shares of the REIT should rise in the market. This was the experience during the period from 1969 through 1972, but in the last couple of years the picture has begun to change. A slump in the construction industry caused by tight money, inflation, and material shortages, coupled with business recession and tenant defaults, has caused havoc in the mortgage REIT community. Without the mortgage payments coming in to meet their own payments on the money they borrowed, many have been unable to meet their commitments when due, which in turn has led to suspended dividends to shareholders and plummeting share prices. When lured by the high returns offered by REITs, think carefully about the real risks involved in this type of leverage.

SUMMARY

The foregoing descriptions of places you can lend your money is not intended to be complete. You must be able to identify something as a loan, understand the risks involved, and calculate the True Rate of Return. Looked at rationally, there is little way a person can lend out money in an inflationary economy and come out ahead; it is almost a certain loss. The loss is gradual, almost unnoticed in many cases. If you lend out $1,000 and get back $1,500 later, it *seems* as though you're doing well, even if you have to give $250 to Uncle Sam. But the valid way to look at the transaction is not how many dollars do I have, but how much purchasing power. As time and the economy progresses you're going to find that purchasing power fading in frightening leaps. The rational position to take is that times have changed. What used to be conservative money management today is suicide. Stay away from debt securities. When you sell a piece of property and are tempted to take back a note for part of the purchase price, try another negotiation to get the cash, even if it's discounted. When someone tells you about the "fantastic" 10% yield on a bond or bank account, give him a short course in True Rate of Return technology. In other words, *get out of legal tender.*

EQUITIES

THE STOCK MARKET

You must have the impression by now that everything in your life that has to do with accumulating wealth relates to inflation. You'll continue to experience this truth; fiat money is the arch-enemy of financial security. As we begin to talk about the stock market, the spectre of inflation will again haunt every decision you make and influence the future of all the stocks you buy. Let's examine how the marketplace and thus the stocks of businesses that comprise the marketplace react to the introduction of fiat money.

The marketplace is comprised of the producers of goods, the distributors of goods, and the consumers of goods. In order to have a high standard of living, someone must produce the items that are to be consumed. Since the producer has only one reason for this production, and that is to make a profit, all his business decisions will be based on estimates of how his decisions will affect profits. In turn, the stockholder is relying on the correctness of the decisions of the operator of the company, due to their effect on the price of the stock and the dividends.

What are the factors that the businessman must cope with when making market decisions? There are three major inputs into the producer: *Materials, Labor,* and *Capital.* Utilizing these inputs the producer assembles his product and offers it to the consumer on a supply-demand basis. If inflation is going to affect the producer and his profits (and thus the value of the shares of his business), it must come through one or all of the inputs mentioned.

Material: The companies and individuals that supply the raw materials and components to a producer are in themselves producers. The effects of inflation on them are the same as on the producer, but still they pass on the effects once again. As the money supply is inflated the costs of materials rise. This causes difficulties in planning for the producer and, consequently, his risk of failure increases. If he doesn't price his end product correctly he may find himself in red ink when the materials cost increases.

Because of the effects of inflation, suppliers are frequently unable to meet the demand of the producer for materials. This is especially true when the government, in response to the cries of the public to do something about inflation, institutes wage and price controls. Suddenly the supplier of the raw materials finds it unprofitable to sell at the government's official price, and the producer's source dries up, or he must buy at a higher-than-normal price through the black market. These supplier complications make survival difficult in business, and increase the ultimate cost to the consumer.

Labor: Labor is another form of material supplied to the producer. In an inflationary economy the labor market demands higher and higher wages to offset increased living costs, without exchanging more time or efficiency in their operation. In a simple society the only reason wages would rise would be if the productive ability of the individual laborer increased. And consequently he would never find it necessary to strike for higher wages, as his standard of living would be increasing without an increase on wages due to the increasing ability of technology to produce more and more consumer goods with the same amount of human labor.

A society without labor strife would reward its citizens with a higher standard of living, as every day a laborer is off work due to a strike (or working at less than full capacity due to a feeling that he's not getting what he's worth), less goods are available. The disruption of the labor force by inflation leads to similar problems for the producer that the rising costs and interrupted supplies from his materials suppliers caused. Again he has lost efficiency due to friction that causes the product he sells to cost the consumer more and causes him to endure a higher degree of risk.

Capital: The producer must go to the capital market in

order to fund expansion of his business activities. In an
inflationary society the producer offsets many of the
negative effects of increasing prices for supplies and labor by
a higher degree of production efficiency, and this he achieves
through an ever expanding investment in the improvement of
his productive mechanism. He absorbs a great deal of the
increasing costs of materials and labor through this means
and thus doesn't have to pass these costs on to the consumer.
But somewhere along the line the cost of these improvements
must be paid for, and this is done through either borrowing
or by selling off part of the business. Even in a non-inflationary
society this process of expansion exists, and there is constant
demand for money to supply the expansion of the producers.
As inflation proceeds it becomes more and more risky to be
an entrepreneur and produce, it becomes more and more
difficult to plan expansion and make it profitable, and more
and more difficult to predict future sales and profits. Since
the profits of business fluctuate due to inflation, the returns
on capital fluctuate as well.

The investors, seeking to put their capital to work in a way
that will overcome inflation, look at a business with more
than an eye to the annual dividend. They want interest on
the use of their money, but more than that they want the
value of their original capital to be protected against the
depreciating effects of inflation. That the company continues
to pay the same dividend every year becomes less important
than that it begins to expand its operations and thus its
future potential earnings. A company that simply earns 10%
per year on its invested capital will not be attractive to the
investor. His drive for growth is a result of subtle forces: like
the inability to make an ever-increasing income raise his
standard of living as much as it seems it should; or watching
and hearing stories of great speculative successes. Even current
tax laws which tax dividends at a less favorable rate than
capital appreciation add to this search for "growth" com-

panies. The producers, if they want to attract capital, must show an increasing expansion, a dynamic growth. This means taking risks and expanding into an unknown, unpredictable future.

Borrowing for investment is a logical phenomenon that accompanies all inflations. The investor, sensing the increasing prices of almost everything, recognizes that he can borrow money today at interest rates that seem to lag behind the pace of inflation, save half the cost of interest through taxes, and thus leverage his profits just on the basis of rising prices. Borrowing becomes psychologically easy because he knows his wages are going up, and that should give him the surplus to meet the new debts. More money feeding into the capital market must find a place to grow, and its availability creates a supply of entrepreneurs willing to start new businesses. Like a self fulfilling prophecy, the search for growth companies stimulates the development of growth companies.

The periods of the 1920's and 1960's in this country are good examples of this. The demand for growth stocks created a flood of new issues. Hardly was a new company formed with any name that indicated growth industry that the stock wasn't over-subscribed before it hit the street. The prices doubled and tripled on these new issues without the buyers as much as knowing the products the company would make, let alone the quality of the management or their ability to operate a long-term, profit-making enterprise. Just the word "new issue" was all that was necessary.

So the cycle runs on. The businessman in order to get capital must offer growth. The capital in order to survive must seek growth. Growth means risk, and the market seems to build in its own downfall. But while it's going on no one can seem to lose, and speculation becomes the craze. There is no better example of this inflation-caused sequence of events than the experience of France in the period immediately following the French revolution. Andrew Dickson White, in his book *Fiat Money Inflation in France*, described the phenomena:

> "A still worse outgrowth [of the currency inflation] was the increase of speculation and gambling. With the plethora of paper currency in 1791 appeared the first evidences of that cancerous disease which always follows large issues of irredeemable currency—a disease more permanently injurious to a nation than war, pestilence or famine. For at the great metropolitan centers grew a luxurious, speculative, stock-gambling body, which like a malignant tumor, absorbed into itself the strength of the nation and sent out its cancerous fibres to the remotest hamlets. At these city centers abundant wealth seemed to be piled up: in the country at large there grew a dislike of steady labor and a contempt for moderate gains and simple living."

As freshly printed money continues to flow into the capital market, as well as into the hands of the consumers who create the demand for the end products, a structure of instability is created. The slightest constriction of credit and the marginal businesses, those entrepreneurs that really weren't suited and qualified to start businesses (and wouldn't have been able to get the capital to do so in an economy where those funds would have to come from the hard earned savings of a producer), will fall, consumer demand for all products will taper off, and even the well-run businesses will falter as their inflation induced expansion plans become unprofitable. Remember the go-go stocks of the sixties and the growth-by-acquisition conglomerates? The whole thing adds up to that misunderstood phenomenon called the business cycle. Evidence is now almost overwhelming that monetary inflation leads to the business cycle, and consequently to the cyclical nature of the stock market. Inflation of the money supply leads to business boom, and business recession; the amplitude of the market swings increase as the inflation progresses. Since monetary inflation cannot seem to reverse itself once the policy of fiat money is established, greater and greater issues of currency are required to sustain the distortions, much like greater and greater amounts of a drug are needed to produce a high, until the economy is totally hooked and the only way out is the pain of withdrawal or death. Constantino Bresciana-Turroni in his book *The Economics of Inflation*[20] described the consequences of a rapidly inflating money supply on the capital market in Germany in 1920 and 1921:

> "It was observed in Germany, as also, indeed, elsewhere, that the circle of speculators was greatly enlarged. Shares were held by speculators in a much larger measure than formerly, when they for the most part had been held longer by investors, who considered them as permanent investments. But in 1920 and 1921 shares passed rapidly from hand to hand, and oscillations of their prices were much more frequent and more violent than formerly . . . It was in the autumn of 1921 that business on the German Bourse reached such a condition as to put in the shade even the classical examples of the most violent fever of speculation."

Anyone who has been confused by the movements of stock prices on the U.S. exchanges over the past ten years could well understand them in light of the experiences of other countries that have undergone inflation.

We had a period of rather sustained upward growth in prices from 1959 to 1965. Now the oscillations have begun. No real forward movement any longer, just up and down to nowhere.

I think that one of the most damaging and most costly illusions that has ever been accepted by the American public is the concept that the stock market will go up and up forever. Almost all mutual fund sales literature has pushed graphs of the past, mountain charts as they call them, which showed the growth of the value of the shares of the mutual funds over the last twenty, thirty or forty years. The insinuation was clear; that trends tend to continue and the great productive power of the United States industrial machine would cause stock prices to continue that upward spiral forever. Millions of people, believing the charts, and believing the fervent sales pitch of the brokerage industry, have been whiplashed into poverty by the violent market fluctuations of the past few years. Yet very few really understood why that growth trend did not continue, and many still have faith it will start again.

The Future

We are at a point where the past cannot repeat itself. The action of the stock market over the next twenty years will *not* be a repeat of the past: it will most certainly follow the classical lines of the capital market of every past society that has seen fit to plunder the future through inflation of the money supply.

What is the most probable course of market action over the next year? Over the next five years? Over the next 20 years? The market in general will be responsive to the real profitability of the companies whose stock makes up the market. And the profitability of these companies will depend on the economic course of the nation as a whole. If we make the assumption that the bureaucrats who make the laws and determine the extent to which the money supply is expanded will continue to make the same mistakes as in the past; that is that they will continue to spend more money on social programs than they are able to collect in taxes, that they will continue to try to solve business recession by expansion of bank credit, that they will continue to react to inflation by blaming the businessman and the consuming public, and therefore slap more and greater controls on the producers to hold prices in line, then we can make some further assumptions about the future course of the capital market.

1. It will become difficult to isolate the true profits
of the companies studied.

2. Profits will be harder to obtain due to increased costs of operation (i.e., increased accounting and legal costs as businessmen try to cope with mounting control programs). Although it will be more and more difficult to make real profits, many companies will appear to be making profits when they are not. They'll be able to do that by camouflaging (perhaps unwittingly) the true costs of depreciating equipment, by not anticipating the future increased costs of supplies and labor, by not properly anticipating the current effects of inflation.

3. Producers will find it harder and harder to obtain the supplies and materials they need on a predictable basis.

4. Shortages, rationing, and black markets will be common byproducts of the bureaucratic interference with the producers' free market.

You might look at this whole mess something like a chicken coop full of laying hens. While they are supplied with the things they need (water and feed) and left alone, they produce at maximum efficiency. But let their supplies become sporadic; go in periodically and try to shake an extra egg out of one and stop another from laying; let a fox loose in the coop; and you'll have total chaos. Egg production will go down. The producers of the products we consume will be no different. Let the government bureaucrats threaten their very lives with antitrust suits, confiscatory taxes, mandatory racial mixes of employees, price controls and wage controls, and you *must* have lower production, higher costs, and a lower standard of living for everyone.

As this book is being written the Dow Jones Industrial Stock average stands below 600, which is in my opinion near the lower end of the cycle. Since inflation produces oscillations in the market the up and down movement can be potentially profitable for the knowledgeable speculator.

To Market, To Market

Let's look at the alternative methods of investing in common stocks:

1. Buy stocks and hold them for the long pull.
2. Trade common stocks, selling those that stop performing as growth stocks and rebuying others. Try to outguess the market but stay invested in stocks.
3. Buy a portfolio of stocks as the market in general appears to be in a rising phase, and sell the entire portfolio when the market appears ready to decline.

You must, in cases one and two, be able to select the best individual companies from the thousands available, and you must believe in a long term rising market. In case number three you must have some system for determining when the market is rising and falling. In other words, the *issue* and the *cycle.*

Selecting the Issue

There are approximately 2000 stocks listed on the New York Stock Exchange, 1250 on the American Exchange, and 2700 on the national over the counter. Add in the regional exchanges and over-the-counter stocks and the total comes to somewhat over 10,000.

The prices of each of these stocks varies according to the potential buyer's assessment of what other buyers might be willing to pay in the future. Factors that go into the determination of future worth are:

1. Financial condition of the company.
2. Ability of the management team.
3. Present and estimated future competitive position of the company's product in the market.
4. Future earnings of the company.
5. An estimate of the future course of the market in general.

One of the first considerations is the reliability of the inputs used for selecting the stock. There is a tremendous bias

present throughout the industry. The owners and managers
of a corporation have a vested interest in seeing that the price
of that stock rises. All financial statements to whatever
extent possible will always be slanted toward the positive. All
news releases will be edited to be as favorable as possible.
Everyone involved has a direct monetary interest in making
that company and its future look good.

Next in line comes the brokerage house that sells the
stock. How much of the stock is held by the brokerage
firm for its own account? How much has been sold to fav-
ored customers in the past? How much is held by the officers and friends of officers in the firm? All these factors
will most certainly influence the statements and recommendations made by a firm to its brokers, and after all,
a broker working for a brokerage firm usually takes his
recommendations from the people for whom he works.
If he doesn't, then his recommendations must be the result
of his own investigations into the value of the stock. What
are his inputs? Has he the time to personally investigate
the company, its management, the market for its products,
etc.? Probably not.

I certainly don't believe that everyone involved is bound to
pass on erroneous information in order to serve his own
interests, but the bias that *must* be injected into this system
by the personal interests of the people involved *tends* to lead
the investor down the wrong paths. When looking for outside
advice, there are two questions that must be answered
(whether that advice is about a medical problem, an
engineering problem, or an investment decision): is the
advisor knowledgeable, and is the advisor self-interested. If he
tends to profit more from giving one recommendation than
another, the tendency will be to give the one that's most
profitable. All the investment areas that might be profitable
for the investor but aren't remunerative for the broker are
left unexplored and undeveloped. Brokers aren't dishonest,
they are blinded by self-interest; a natural human frailty.

If you're going to select an individual stock, then, whose

advice do you take? My personal view, after having been
involved directly in the capital market for many years, is that
the average individual is not able to make rational informed
decisions about individual stocks whether his advice comes
from himself or his stock broker. To do so on his own would
mean he would have to have access to reliable information
about the affairs of the companies, the industries in which
they operate, and the economic outlook as a whole.

From your standpoint as an investor, you must steer a
course around these pitfalls, and the best way to do that is by
taking your advice from someone who does not stand to
profit from the investment he makes for you, but only from
being right in that advice.

It's unfortunate that the regulatory bodies that are charged
with protecting the public from the abuses of unethical
practitioners set up rules and regulations that preclude the
ethical practitioner from being properly compensated. For
example, if there is a mutual fund for sale and the
commission rate that that fund pays to the salesman is 8%,
the investment advisor either must take a fee for his services
and forego the commission, or take a commission and forego
the fee. He can't take a commission and rebate it to the
buyer, which is what he should do. So if you want to pay a
fee to an advisor, you'll wind up paying a commission to
someone else, whether you like it or not. The result is that
the investor avoids the fee advisor and takes his advice from
the commission salesman. Once you start buying from him,
how can he be objective about his advice if his entire income
is dependent on the investments he recommends?

The point is clear. If you want advice, don't seek it from a
salesman. He'll steer you to his own product. Seek it from an
independent advisor, someone who will stand to benefit if
the advice is sound and will stand to lose if the advice is
unsound. About the only person you probably know who
fills this bill is yourself, and more likely than not, you're
unqualified to render the advice to yourself. You have the

integrity to treat yourself honestly, but you may not have the knowledge. If you refuse to take the time to make yourself knowledgeable, then the next best step would be to find an advisor and arrange to pay him provided his advice is correct and collect damages from him if it's not.

The closest thing to both knowledgeability and coincidence of interest would be a managed account in which an independent advisor, for a fee, advises as to which stocks to buy. Make sure there is no opportunity for that person to benefit by recommending one stock over another or by churning the account. Furthermore, there should be some relationship between the performance of the recommended stocks and the income to the advisor (the idea of having the advisor be penalized if performance is not up to standard has not been tried). Obviously positive or negative remuneration based on the performance of the portfolio will not guarantee results, but its effect would be to weed out the advisors that weren't competent, as they wouldn't be able to make a living and would quickly migrate to other occupations.

Managed Portfolios

Since one of the most logical (at least in my opinion) methods of investing in the stock market is through hiring an independent advisor and paying him for selecting individual stock issues, the managed portfolio might be one of the more obvious avenues to consider. The theory behind a managed portfolio is that a group of people with more or less similar financial objectives pool their money and hire a portfolio manager. Due to the large amount of money available, the portfolio manager is able to hire a staff of people. These might include financial analysts that would concentrate on studying the various industry groups, chartists that would plot the movements of individual securities, selling and buying order specialists that would assure the best prices once a stock selection was made.

Assuming that the manager was remunerated based on a

flat fee (most mutual funds charge their shareholders
somewhere between 1/10th of 1% and 1½% of the average
asset value of the fund per year as a management fee), then
his advice should be relatively objective. Without a doubt it's
far more objective than taking the same stock recommendations from someone who was compensated based on the
number of sales and purchases within the portfolio. Additionally, by pooling resources a great deal more weight can be
swung in the investment world. Doors open for access to
inside information far more readily when an investor is
representing $10,000,000 than when he's representing
$10,000. Furthermore, access to the more sophisticated tools
of stock analysis such as computers is certainly limited to the
big spenders. Assuming you feel like you'd like the effects of
pooling your funds with those of others in order to hire a
portfolio manager, there are several alternatives available.

Bank Trusts. Bank trusts operate in a manner similar to
mutual funds. The bank hires portfolio managers to buy and
sell common stocks and other securities for its common trust
fund. Many banks will set up several different funds, each
catering to the particular needs of its clients, such as a growth
fund, an income fund, etc. Unlike the mutual funds, the
historical data about the performance of these funds is not as
easy to come by, and is not available on a daily basis in your
local newspaper. Additionally, by reason of their affiliation
with the bank, these funds are attractive to unsophisticated
widows and orphans whose money was left via wills naming
the bank as trustee. The banks' byword is conservatism; they
would far rather forego a potential profit than risk a loss.
This may be prudent management in an economy that
doesn't suffer from the inflation rampant in this country, but
today, limiting oneself to preservation of the original capital
means certain loss. The bank gets paid whether the individual
makes a profit or not, and since the typical investor in a bank
trust never pays much attention to the comparative results of
the trust versus other managed portfolios, the banker feels

the safest route is the route of no growth and no apparent loss. Bank trusts in general should be avoided.

Investment Advisors. There are quite a number of investment advisors who will manage money in the market for a fee. In these cases you commit a certain amount of capital (the minimums vary from advisor to advisor, with the lowest being about $10,000, but the average minimum being closer to $25,000), and the advisor then purchases stock for you in your name. Thus you own a series of individual issues. In theory the advisor tailors the portfolio to suit your individual needs and preferences. He may submit recommendations to you for your approval prior to purchase, or may have discretion to buy and sell as he sees fit.

Technically this concept is preferable to the idea of a bank trust, but the problems are that unless you have a great deal of capital you can't diversify very well, and second there is usually no reliable record available which would indicate how well the advisor has done in the past. It should be obvious that most advisors don't tailor accounts exactly to the specifications of the individuals involved, but must lump investors into categories such as need for growth, conservation of capital, etc. Calculating the fee an advisor would get from an account of say $25,000 (which might amount to $750 per year) would tell you that he really couldn't afford to pay too much attention to your particular problems. Since these accounts are not bound by as strict rules for accounting, record keeping, etc. as are more public vehicles like mutual funds, you will never know how badly he may have managed other clients' funds. Additionally there is opportunity for an independent advisor to take under-the-table kickbacks from the brokers through which he places his buy and sell orders. This would create the conflict of interest that you are trying to avoid.

Mutual Funds. The third category of managed portfolios is the mutual fund. Today there are over 500 mutual funds in operation, including open-end funds, closed-end funds and duo-funds. Since a mutual fund is a logical investment vehicle, I'm going to take some time to explain how they function, and how to avoid some of the more common pitfalls of investing in them.

An open-end mutual fund is a pool of shareholders' money which is invested in a portfolio of securities at the discretion of the manager of the fund. The structure and sequence of events is diagrammed in Figure 14. Shareholders contribute to the pool and receive shares in return proportionate to their relative investment. In other words, if 1,000 investors each invested $1,000 there would be a total contribution of $1,000,000. If the fund initially decided to price its shares at $10 then they would issue 10,000 shares and each investor would receive 100 shares. As new shareholders were added new shares would be issued, but the addition or deletion of new shareholders *would not in itself change the share price of the fund.* For example, if another 1,000 investors contributed another $1,000 apiece the fund would simply issue an additional 10,000 shares at $10 a share and each shareholder would own the same proportionate share of the total assets of the fund.

The money is not sent directly to the manager of the fund, but rather the manager selects an independent trustee, usually a major bank or trust company, and this trustee receives and cares for the money, for which it is paid a fee, of course. The fund management has no immediate access to the funds and merely instructs the trustee as to the stocks it should buy and sell. When the trustee places a purchase order, the stock certificates are returned to it, and it holds them in safekeeping.

When dividends are received, the trustee deducts the costs of administration, as well as the management fee for the management company, and the balance is sent to the shareholders as a taxable distribution. When the management company directs the trustee to sell a stock held in the portfolio, that stock is sold and the proceeds are reinvested

The Structure of A Mutual Fund

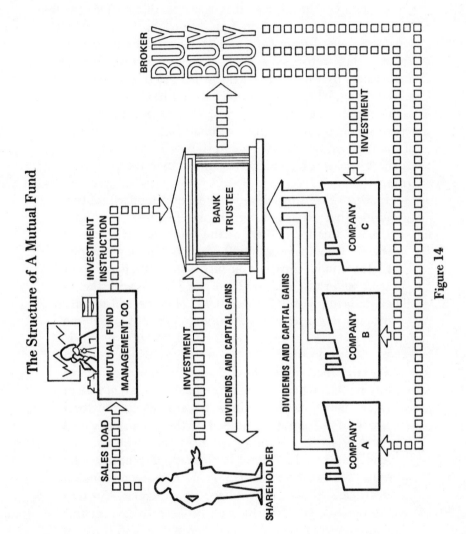

Figure 14

or held in interest bearing securities at the direction of the managers of the fund. If a gain is realized on the sale of a stock held by the fund, that gain is distributed to the shareholders of the fund on a prorata basis. It is identified as a capital gain distribution and is reportable on the shareholders' tax returns as such. Usually a cash reserve is maintained by the funds with which to meet shareholder redemptions. When a shareholder wishes to cash out, he sends in his certificates to the fund, they are retired, and he receives a check for his proportionate share of the net assets of the fund on the day of redemption.

There are several categories of mutual funds to choose from.

1. **Open-End Load Funds.** These are standard mutual funds that charge a fee for buying into the fund. Usually this fee is 8½% of the total cost of the fund shares, which amounts to 9.3% of the money you pay to the fund. Thus if you buy a share that has a net asset value of $10.00, you'll pay $10.93, with the 93 cents being 8½% of the $10.93. This fee will usually drop as larger amounts are invested until it gets down to about 1% for investments of $1,000,000 or more.

2. **No-Load Funds.** These are funds which act just like the load funds but charge little or no fee for buying in. When you buy a share it is at net asset value, which is determined by adding up the total assets of the fund at the end of the trading day and dividing by the number of shares outstanding. The load paid to a load fund is normally disbursed to the sales organization to compensate the commission salesman. No-load funds have no salesmen, but rely on newspaper and other advertising to sell shares. Although they tend to be smaller in size than the load funds, and there are fewer of them, their performance does not seem to be adversely affected by their lack of commissioned salesmen.

3. Closed-End Funds. Most of the funds on the market are so-called open-end investment companies. Open-end refers to the continuous sale and redemption of shares by the fund. A closed-end fund is a pool of investors' money the same as the open-end fund, but in this case the fund issues a fixed number of shares and then closes off the sale. Nor does it redeem shares from shareholders should they desire to liquidate their holdings. A shareholder who wishes to sell must find an outside buyer, just as must the holder of shares in an individual corporation. Shares in closed-end funds, therefore, are sold through brokerage houses and these companies are usually listed as over-the-counter stocks.

Since sale of shares and purchase of shares after the fund has ceased selling is done at arm's length between two investors, the shares do not necessarily sell for net asset value but will normally sell at a premium or a discount. This means that if a fund holds shares of stock valued at $1,000,000 and is selling at a 15% discount, you could buy all the shares of the fund for $850,000. Closed-end funds frequently sell at discounts up to 30% of net asset value. Most brokers don't push closed-end funds because they carry commissions at the same rate that individual stocks do, rather than the more attractive load-fund rates.

4. Dual Purpose Funds. These are a variation on the closed-end funds in which there are two classes of shares. Initially half the shares of the fund are sold as preferred or income shares, and half sold as capital or equity shares. The income shares receive all the dividend income from the stocks held in the portfolio, and the capital shares receive all the capital gains. Thus, if the income investors put up half the capital, they get double the income they normally

would, while the capital shares receive double the
capital gains they normally would. These funds are
usually set up to close out and redeem all shares at
asset value at some predetermined date in the future.
Thus, even though the shares may be currently selling
at a discount, the buyer can be assured the discount
will be eliminated if he holds the shares to maturity.

Most actively traded mutual funds are listed daily in the
Wall Street Journal and most major newspapers around the
country. Open-end funds are listed under Mutual Funds, and
there are separate headings for Closed-End Funds and
Dual-Purpose Funds. No-load funds can be distinguished in
the open-end fund listing by looking at the two prices listed.
If the Net Asset Value (NAV) and the Asked or Purchase
(Prc.) price are the same, then it's a no-load.

If you believe that you're not qualified to select individual
issues, and that you probably can't find a broker that will
objectively handle that chore for you, yet you want to use
the stock market as a vehicle for your equity assets, then a
mutual fund is probably for you.

Strategies

Assuming you study the variety of funds available and
choose one that seems best suited, then you arrive at the
decision of what strategy you'll use in terms of when to buy
and when to sell. As mentioned earlier, there are three basic
strategies that can be used.

1. **Buy and hold for the long pull, adding new money
as it becomes available.** This strategy would have
worked admirably for you had you started into
mutual funds thirty or forty years ago. Hardly a fund
in existence for that time would have done less than
12% per year compounded. Unfortunately history
and common sense economics would indicate that
those days are gone forever. The person that invests
in this manner today may find his total assets

twenty years from now less than the total money he
has invested along the way.

2. Try and find the "hot" fund. When it gets cold,
switch to another. This strategy implies that you can
find that hot fund, and that you can determine when
it's getting cold. There are a variety of theories that
have been developed to do just that. Richardson and
Roebuck put out a booklet called *Choosing a Mutual
Fund for Maximum Growth*.[21] They developed four
guideposts for this task as follows:

> Guidepost No. 1: For maximum growth,
> invest in a mutual fund with total assets of
> only a few million dollars—preferably under
> $50 million and certainly no more than $150
> million.
>
> Guidepost No. 2: For maximum growth,
> invest in a mutual fund that's enjoying a
> substantial influx of new money.
>
> Guidepost No. 3: For maximum growth,
> invest in a mutual fund with proven manage-
> ment.
>
> Guidepost No. 4: For maximum growth,
> invest in a mutual fund that maintains an
> appropriate cash position.

One of the most obvious problems in this strategy is
that even if you select from the top 10% of the funds
in a rising market, you'll still be invested in funds when
the market falls. If you believe that the overall long
run trend of the market is not up, but rather sideways,
then you have to do considerably better in up
markets than in down markets to come out ahead.

3. Determine the market trends. Go into funds when
the market is rising and get out and into cash or
bonds when it is falling. If you believe that the
market is a place in which to have a portion of your
assets working, that you can't effectively select

individual issues, and that the market will fluctuate up and down in cycles due to fiat-money inflation, this third strategy might be your best bet. The obvious difficulty in succeeding at this in-and-out technique is to be able to correctly predict the market swings. To say it's difficult is to magnificently understate the problem.

MARKET TREND INDICATORS

Charting the market is one technique by which market swings can sometimes be predicted. The question is, is the past performance of the market a key to the future performance? Probably, but who has the magic glasses to read through the unimportant data and filter out the causal factors? Are the streets wet because it rained, or did it rain because the streets are wet? When two events seem to always accompany each other there can frequently be confusion about the cause and the effect. When you have hundreds of events, all intertwined, and all subjectively evaluated, it may be impossible. One of the most entertaining and enjoyable books on the whole subject of selecting stocks, and the methods of doing so, is Burton G. Malkiel's *A Random Walk Down Wall Street*.[22] Before you subscribe to any method, be it charting, fundamental analysis, or hemline watching, you should read it.

S-4/B-1 Switching System

One method of moving in and out of the market without trying to predict its trends is simply to move into the market when it is going up and move out when it is headed down. Anyone can avoid a loss greater than 5% at any point by simply deciding to sell his stocks if they move down that amount. One of the more interesting and historically profitable systems in this regard is played with the Keystone S-4 common stock fund and Keystone B-1 bond fund.

It seems that the market moves in cycles, and Keystone S-4 is an old time mutual fund that is representative of the market as a whole. It invests in low-priced common stocks, and unlike other mutual funds it does not attempt to go into a cash position when the market is falling, but remains fully invested in stocks. Adapting a strategy of following the 39-week moving average of the Dow-Jones 30-Industrials to indicate market cycles, we plotted the 39-week-moving-average price of Keystone S-4 against its weekly closing price for the last five years. Under the assumption that the market was going to continue indefinitely through a series of oscillations, it was determined that during periods that the closing price of S-4 was above its 39-week average price, funds would be invested in S-4, and when the weekly price fell below the 39-week moving average price, the shares of S-4 would be sold and the money switched to Keystone B-1, a high quality bond fund. By switching back and forth, the investment would be in stocks during up markets and bonds during periods of decline. Figure 15 shows the five year curves and indicates points of change. Had $100,000 been invested initially and stayed in S-4 during the entire five year period from September 1, 1969 to August 31, 1974 it would have had a redemption value of $42,000. Had it been moved back and forth according to the system it would have had an ending value of $105,000.

If this seems like a small gain in comparison even to a savings account, you should realize that it was achieved playing a stock market strategy in one of the worst markets since the depression. If the market climbed back to its starting point at the beginning of the period, the results would be   out-standing.

In actual practice the system has certain dangers. First, there is a tendency to second guess the market. When a crossing point occurs it often seems as though the market is about to reverse itself, and one becomes unwilling to make the switch. Second, if there is a double signal, a cross and

S-4/B-1 Switching System

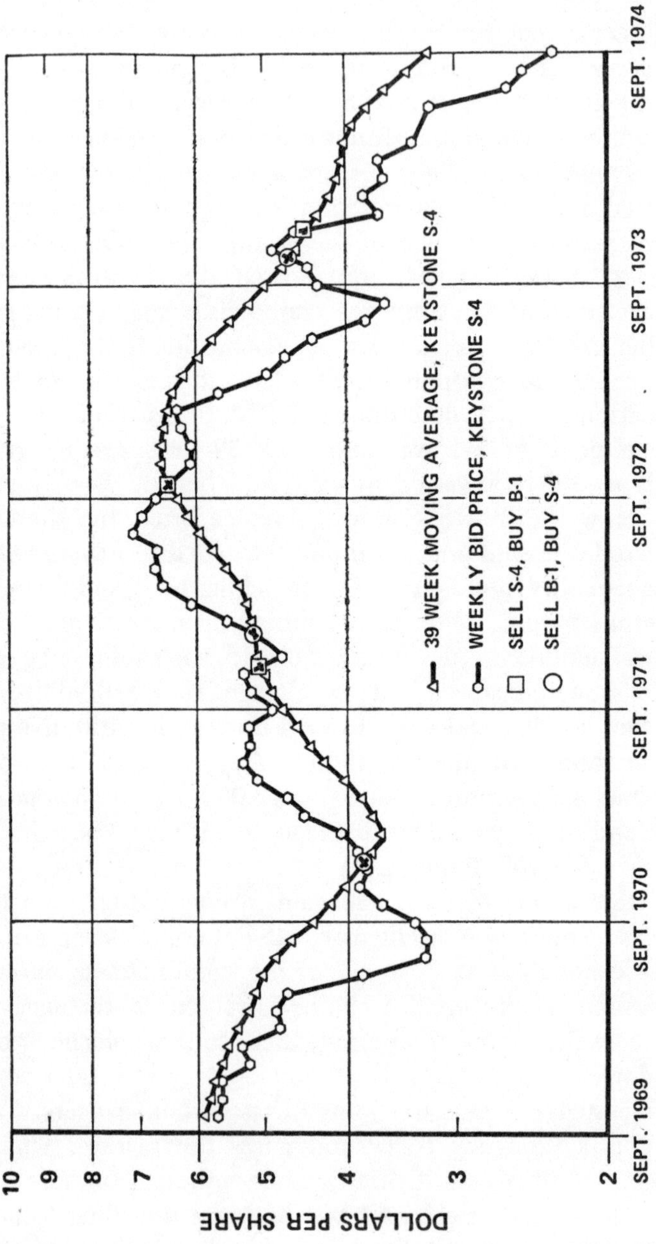

39 WEEK MOVING AVERAGE, KEYSTONE S-4
WEEKLY BID PRICE, KEYSTONE S-4
☐ SELL S-4, BUY B-1
○ SELL B-1, BUY S-4

Figure 15

then a re-cross, the cost for switching becomes a significant loss. S-4 is a load fund, and even though B-1 is part of the same family of funds, the management company still charges a load for making any conversion. Converting from one fund to another usually costs half the normal fee for the dollar value transferred, unless the money has been in the first fund for less than 90 days, in which case they charge a full load.

Nevertheless, even with the fees paid for all crosses, it is obvious that at least during the five year period studied, one would have been much better off moving back and forth from bonds to stocks rather than remaining invested in stocks. It would be possible, of course, to play the same basic system using a no-load fund, and going to cash when a signal came to get out of the market. The studies indicate, however, that S-4 is still better, even with the load, because of the peculiar nature of the fund. It remains fully invested in stocks even when the market is low, so the fund loses no profits when the market does turn upward. Other funds that may be partially in cash during a down market will require some time to become invested again, and thus will lose the gains they could have made had their funds been invested fully at the turning point.

Another factor that affects the profitability of the system is the amount invested. In the illustration we invested $100,000 in the fund, which results in a conversion fee of 1% from S-4 to B-1, and 1.875% from B-1 to S-4. Smaller amounts of money invested would result in substantially higher fees for switching and would diminish the beneficial effects of the system. Additionally, there is nothing to prevent the market from starting a series of rapid oscillations that would carry the weekly closing price back and forth across the 39-week moving average line, and trigger a number of switches in a short period of time. Depending on the amount of money being switched, this could be costly.

So much for the S-4/B-1 system. Properly handled it could be one tool for an investor that would enable him to take

advantage of market upswings without getting caught in any
major market declines.

Monetarism

Another concept of investing which has to do with
switching in and out of mutual funds (or any portfolio of
common stocks) has grown out of the monetarist school of
economics. There has been a belief among these economists
that the supply of money is directly related to the business
cycle. If true, and if a relationship between the business cycle
and the level of stock prices can be established, then increases
or decreases in the money supply would directly influence
the price of stocks. Dr. Beryl Sprinkel first analyzed this
relationship in his 1964 book *Money and Stock Prices* and
then again in 1971 in *Money and Markets: A Monetarist
View*.[23]

Dr. Sprinkel's books are probably most useful for the
financial analyst and not the lay investor. Although written
in a readable style and painstakingly thorough in documenta-
tion, the whole subject of the ways in which the Federal
Reserve directly and indirectly influences the money supply,
and how the money supply in turn influences the course of
business activity, and ultimately the prices of stocks, takes a
great deal of concentration and basic knowledge to follow.

If you as an equity investor are willing to take the time to
understand the significance of the Federal Reserve policies
and either to go to your library or subscribe to their monthly
bulletins, you can no doubt improve your investment results
significantly by timing your stock purchases and sales to
coincide with the market cycles generated by the money
supply fluctuations. If you'd like to try this, get both of Dr.
Sprinkel's books, read them twice, and then make yourself
aware of current Federal Reserve monetary policy by reading
Monetary Trends, the monthly publication of The Federal
Reserve Bank of St. Louis.

If you're not interested in going to that much trouble, just be generally aware that when the Federal Reserve opts for easier money policies to stimulate the economy, it won't be long before business and subsequently stock prices will trend upwards, and when they begin restrictive measures, it won't be long before a decline sets in.

SUMMARY

For the average investor the most practical method of investing in the equities market is through purchase of a mutual fund, preferably a no-load fund. The key to profits is to realize that the long term trend of the market is not up, but rather up and down. To take advantage of this inflationary phenomenon you must be ready to move in and out as the cycles occur, basing your timing on either a simple stop-loss formula like the 39-week moving average of a representative group of stocks, or on some broad economic indicator such as the monetary policy of the Fed. In any case, don't waste your time and endanger your assets unless you're willing to make yourself knowledgeable about what you're doing. Don't walk out and hope that some salesman, or even paid advisor will take the responsibility off your shoulders. You're the only one who has the integrity to handle your money carefully and responsibly. Now just gain the knowledge.

CHAPTER FOUR

Insurance

Risk as I defined it in an earlier chapter means exposure to loss, and insurance represents pooled risk. It's a guarantee that the insured will be reimbursed for certain financial losses when and if they occur. In more primitive societies, when an individual suffers a major loss the neighbors pool their resources to aid that individual. When a farmer's barn burns down the neighbors will hold a "barn-raising." When he's too ill to till his fields they share the burden. Thus the people in the community pool their risks. This is a form of insurance with the premium being the obligation to do the same for others in the community. In today's society insurance is on a monetary basis. When we have an accident we no longer rely on the charity of our neighbors, but rather we contribute in advance to a pool of money, along with many thousands of other individuals, and when catastrophe does strike we are entitled to dip into that pool of money and recover part or all of our loss. An insurance company is in business to make a profit, and by offering you the chance to share your risk with others, it takes a profit for its role in the calculation of that risk.

The profits of the insurance company are determined by a number of factors:

1. How well its actuaries are able to calculate the

number of losses that might occur in given situations and properly charge the subscriber for that risk.

2. How efficiently its operations are able to minimize overhead while properly servicing the client.

3. How successful it is in advertising and promotion and the training of its sales force, in order to sell its product to a great number of people.

WHAT LOSSES SHOULD BE COVERED?

If an unforeseen occurrence could cause you financial loss, then it is possible that this risk should be covered by insurance. To determine when it's necessary, look at the extent of the potential financial loss. If the loss would force you to alter your financial goals or change your standard of living, then you would be wise to cover that risk by insurance. Conversely, *if you can easily pay for the loss out of present assets or earnings without significantly affecting your economic position, then you should probably act as your own insurance company.* You should pay yourself the premiums and thus earn for yourself the salesman's commissions, overhead expense allowance, and profits that would have accrued to them.

An example of this is automobile collision insurance. When you buy collision insurance, the insurance company will determine statistically the number of accidents you'll have and will charge enough to pay for the repairs on the accidents plus commissions. In addition the company will charge you overhead expense and profits. One of my clients, a successful doctor, has a net worth in excess of $500,000. He drives an automobile worth about $9,000 and the automobile has been fully covered by collision insurance for a premium of $110.00 per year. Statistically he will have approximately 0.25 accidents this year and the cost of repairs will be about $50. The balance of the premium will pay the insurance company its operating costs and profits. Assuming that the doctor pays this premium for a period of fifty years (from age 20 to age 70) he will have tripled the cost of repairing his automobile.

The only reason he bothered to insure was habit. Since he could have afforded to pay for any damage without affecting his financial security, he should have done so. The only possible reasons for carrying collision insurance are: 1. You may be financing the car and thus the lending institution may require collision insurance, 2. You may not be able to afford to replace your car if it is damaged.*

This logic regarding the reason to buy insurance applies throughout the field of insurance. *If you can afford to cover a loss yourself, don't pay an insurance company to cover it for you.* You'll probably be playing the insurance game for fifty years; buying it because you think you might "profit" from it is injudicious. You can't profit by buying insurance any more than you can profit by gambling at the roulette wheel at Las Vegas. You may play for a short time and come out a winner, but play long enough and the laws of probability will get you. You'll most certainly lose.

HOW MUCH SHOULD BE CARRIED?

After you determine that you need insurance to cover a risk, you must calculate the size of the potential loss, and thereby determine the amount of insurance needed. Some potential losses are so large it's impossible to insure against them. An example would be the loss caused by a disabling accident or illness. A highly-paid professional might be

---

*In the example about automobile insurance I'm not referring to public liability insurance on the auto. The loss from an injury to another person can be so enormous that few people can afford to cover the risk themselves. If you were sued for half a million dollars after causing an accident, could you pay without damage to your financial security? If not, then insure.

earning $200,000 per year and have twenty or thirty years of earning power ahead. There is no insurance company that I know that would be willing to completely cover that loss. In cases like this it's more practical to look not at the loss, but at the size of the *need* if the loss occurred. The true needs of the individual would normally be far less than the amount of his current income, and therefore it would be sensible to buy enough insurance to cover his needs, rather than his loss. Thus we have another rule that should always be followed: *buy only enough to satisfy the need.*

After you've determined the amount of insurance, you must shop the market to find the companies that offer the best contracts at the lowest price. Insurance contracts are written in carefully worded legal language and are based on past experience of the company and future assumptions of loss. While provisions of certain types of contracts are almost completely dictated by state laws, other types are at the discretion of the company. In life insurance, for example, the majority of the policy provisions are written to conform to the stringent requirements of state insurance codes, and thus the contracts of all companies will be essentially identical. In disability insurance, on the other hand, companies have a much wider latitude in wording and coverage. When the fine print of one disability policy says you are protected from *sickness contracted during the term of the policy,* and another says you are protected from *sickness which first manifests itself during the term of the policy,* you have to be both alert and knowledgeable to realize the significance of the change in wording.

The insurance problem summarized is:

1. Determine need;
2. Compare contracts;
3. Shop price.

As I cover each area of insurance I'll give you information on how to handle these problems.

LIFE INSURANCE

The concept of life insurance has spawned one of the largest industries in the world. Assets of life insurance companies in the United States totaled $252 billion at the end of 1973. There is about $1.75 trillion of coverage in force, which is the equivalent of $8,000 on every man, woman, and child in the country. Yet I would doubt that one insured in a hundred has the correct amount, type, and is paying the lowest premium available to him. The life insurance industry *sells* insurance, people don't *buy* it. The product is so thoroughly camouflaged that few people ever recognize what they're buying.

One clue to the industry lies in your local library. Peruse the books available on salesmanship; you'll find the vast majority were written by life insurance salesmen. Why? Because this is the biggest training ground for salesmen in the world. No industry has ever concentrated so much energy and money in the development of raw sales technique as has the life insurance industry. Whenever any industry relies that heavily on sales technique, you can be sure the customer will have little objective product information. The purpose of the salesman who'll be confronting you is to sell the maximum amount of insurance that you can be induced to buy and to make it the kind that will be the most profitable to him and his company. In very few cases is this the most profitable for you. If you want to buy insurance correctly the *last* person to contact is your life insurance agent. He has been brainwashed by the life insurance industry not to satisfy your need, but to satisfy theirs.

The correct approach to the purchase of life insurance is the same as for any other form of insurance. First determine what *financial* losses will occur upon death of the insured. Then determine what contracts are available and which companies offer the lowest rates for the type and size policy you need.

When Is a "Need" Not a Need?

Here are a few of your needs that the life insurance salesman will point out:

1. Capital to provide an income to the family.
2. Money with which to pay estate taxes.
3. Money to pay off the home mortgage.
4. Money to pay off the installment debts and notes.
5. Money to educate the children.
6. Money to buy out partners in your business.
7. Money for the business to replace your loss as an employee.
8. Money to retire on.
9. In the case of insuring a non-working wife, money to pay the costs of a housekeeper and the increased income taxes due to the loss of the exemption.
10. If you're young, to insure your future insurability.
11. To capture the lower rates only available to younger people.
12. To fund your pension plan or Keogh plan.

Before you accept his word that these are valid needs you'd better examine your own situation thoroughly. In fact, before you even talk to an agent you should make your own calculations. What will be the financial loss to others in the event of your death? This, of course, depends on your situation.

Insuring Children

Let's assume you are considering insuring a child. At this point in the child's life it's probable that no one is dependent on it for support, so if it dies, no one will be deprived of income. The only financial consequences will be the costs of burial, and properly handled these will be minimal. Therefore the only possible insurance need would be the funeral expenses, and then only if they can't be met from existing resources. "Yes" you say, "but the salesman pointed out that I could fund my children's education by buying insurance." Don't confuse insurance with investing even if they are combined by the insurance company. When I talk about insurance need I'm speaking solely of alleviating the *financial loss* of death through the payment of insurance premiums. I'll discuss the idea of using insurance as a vehicle for the accumulation of wealth later in this chapter.

O.K., but what about the idea that you can buy insurance at much lower rates when you're young? At age 5 the rate is only $7.00 per $1,000 of insurance. By the time the child reaches 25 it will have jumped to $12.00 per $1,000 of insurance. Yes it will, but believe it or not the cost *per thousand dollars of coverage* when you reach age 25 will be the same whether the policy is taken out at age 5 and kept until then, or taken out when needed. Since medical science is progressing and life expectancies are increasing, 20 years from now insurance premiums for a 25-year-old will probably be less than they are today. All you will have accomplished by taking out the insurance at age five is to guarantee the right to *have it* at age 25. Paying the full premiums for years when you don't need the insurance is a pretty high price to pay for the guarantee of insurability. I'll shortly prove the point that the cost will not go up if you wait until you're older to buy. The conclusion regarding buying life insurance on children is this: don't waste your money unless you can't afford the burial costs. It's senseless.

Insuring a Non-Income Producing Spouse

How about buying insurance on a non-income producing member of the household whose economic value lies in their contribution to maintenance of the home and care of the family, like a non-working wife? Again the test is simple. What is the economic result of the death of this member of

the family? Can this loss be met from the assets or income of
the remaining family members without undue strain? Typically the person we're referring to is the wife, although it
might be a non-working husband, father, mother or other
person.

If a wife is lost, someone must take over the labor she
performs. It might entail the hiring of a housekeeper, and
babysitters, and could also mean the breadwinner might have
to work less hours. It will certainly mean the loss of an
income tax deduction, and could result in the payment of
inheritance and estate taxes if the estate is sufficiently large.
But let's not forget the financial gains which might offset
part of these losses. The deceased spouse will no longer need
to be fed, clothed, entertained, taken on vacations, cared for
medically, furnished transportation, or lodging. It's doubtful
that there are many cases in which the financial losses would
really exceed the gains. Wives are expensive propositions, as is
the carrying of any member of a household. And even if it
were slightly more expensive to pay for the new costs of
babysitters, housekeepers, etc., there is more than an even
chance that the current income of the working, surviving
spouse would be able to cope with the added expense.

How about the question of estate taxes? Suppose the
couple's gross estate is $300,000. Under the community
property laws, the wife already owns $150,000 worth of the
property. The other $150,000 would be taxable but after the
decedent's $60,000 personal estate tax exemption, only
$90,000 would be subject to tax. This would result in federal
estate taxes of about $18,000 plus administrative and
probate costs (depending on the way in which title to the
property had been held), and any state inheritance taxes.
Any life insurance salesman worth his license would sell a
whole life policy in this case to cover the entire amount. Yet
the real question is, would the reduction of assets caused by
payment of the taxes really diminish the survivor's wealth in
a way that would make him or her unable to meet goals as

scheduled? Remember, the only reason to buy insurance is to cover a financial risk that you can't afford to cover any other way.

A family should carefully examine its need to insure the non-working members. They'll usually come to the conclusion that it's unnecessary. Take the premium that would have been spent for that non-working member, and invest it; the great probability is that that member won't die anyway, and the premium dollars will come in very handy at retirement.

Insuring the Breadwinner

The obvious purpose of life insurance is to provide funds with which to meet the obligations that normally would be paid out of income if the person producing that income dies. These include:

1. Debts.
2. The obligation of continuing support for dependents.
3. The costs of death including taxes and burial.

Figure 16 is a sample calculation format for determining how much life insurance to carry. By filling in the "Needs" column and the "Assets" column, the net insurance required can be arrived at.

Covering the Debts. To determine the amount of insurance that should be carried, first determine the size of these obligations. Let's take them one at a time beginning with debts. Add up all outstanding notes and accounts. The mortgages on real estate may be excluded inasmuch as these are not debts in the same sense that an account at a department store is a debt. The home itself is an asset, even though it may have an outstanding mortgage, and shouldn't be considered a liability.

A decision should be made as to whether the surviving spouse will continue to live in the home. If the answer is no, then the *net equity* in the home should be listed under

"Assets" and the assumption made that the home will be sold and the proceeds from the sale will become part of the general assets. If the survivor intends to buy another home, either for cash or with a down payment, the amount of cash required should be listed as a need. When calculating the income needed for the family, a provision would then be made for the annual cost of the dwelling.

If the wife is going to remain in the present home, she has the alternative of paying off the mortgage or continuing to make monthly payments. A payoff would be entered as a cash need. If she continues mortgage payments the amount of the payment is part of her need for income and capital must be provided to meet that income need. From the standpoint of life insurance need, if the wife stays in the home it is inconsequential whether she pays off the mortgage or not. One way she needs the capital to pay it off, the other way she needs the capital to provide the income necessary to continue making the payments on the mortgage.

Final Expenses. Next comes the cost of estate taxes, burial, and other final expenses. The estate tax table in the Appendix should assist you in calculating what these might be. As far as final expenses goes, it's your funeral. Estimate how grand you want that last tribute to your mortal remains to be and enter that figure accordingly. Most dedicated insurance agents will always jack up this figure by throwing in a bit about final medical expenses. I don't agree with this. Your medical costs should be taken care of by medical insurance, not life insurance, and buying extra life insurance to take care of them just doesn't make sense. I suppose if a person were unable to get the kind of medical insurance he needed, it might be a last resort to cover some of this potential loss through life insurance, but you have to die in this case to pay the medical bills. Hardly an incentive for your doctor to cure you.

Family Income. The next, and by far the most difficult, determination to make is how much capital is required to support the dependents after the breadwinner is gone. Here we have to make assumptions about the need for income and the probability of certain future events occurring.

Income can be provided in three ways: From the efforts of work; from charity; or from capital. Either you work, your money works, or you look to charity. Since most people don't want to accept charity, let's look at the other possibilities. If the breadwinner dies, the wife or children could begin to provide income by working. Although this is an individual decision that each family must make, here are a few thoughts that may help. Does the wife have a skill? If not, she could probably develop one within a few years of the death of the spouse by entering some program of education. Will she want to work? If the children are young, perhaps not. Then the husband can simply provide the money to meet the family's income needs. Perhaps she will want to work simply to have something to occupy her time. Assuming a minimal income from this type of effort would be sensible. If the wife is young and childless she would probably remarry. In fact, most young marrieds who have no children should examine carefully the concept of life insurance, as there may be no logical reason to carry it at all. The wife survived some way prior to marriage, and could probably revert to that method of survival in the event of the death of her husband. Since the chances of his death are small, they would normally be better off by spending or saving those premiums.

Don't automatically assume that the wife will remarry or go to work in the event of the husband's death, before considering the chance that she might not be able to do either. For example, there could be an auto accident in which the husband is killed and the wife seriously crippled. Chances are small of this happening to any given family, but it does happen and is worth thinking about.

From your budget sheet you should be able to determine the amount of income that the dependents will need in the

event of the breadwinner's death. Decide how much of that
income can reasonably be expected to come from the efforts
of the survivors; the balance must be provided by the money
left by the deceased.*

A Hypothetical Case. Let's take a hypothetical case and
work it through to help you get an idea of how to calculate
your own need for insurance. Assume a family of four,
husband's age is 35, wife's is 35, two children ages 8 and 10.
There are approximately $8,500 in outstanding debts
including an auto loan, some charge accounts, and a small
loan against the husband's equipment. In addition they figure
they're about $1,000 behind at this point in the year as to
what their total tax bill will be. They have estimated their
final expenses if he were to die at $3,000 (which includes
travel expenses to fly his parents to the funeral). Their estate
taxes and probate-administration fees will probably come to
about $2,000. They live in a home that's worth about
$50,000 with a $32,000 mortgage against it, and if the
husband were to die, the wife would stay in the home. In the
event of the husband's death, the wife would need to pay off
the loans, pay the final expenses, and meet her income needs,
which would include the payment on the home plus the
regular monthly living costs.

Since the children are young but in school, she'll work part
time, taking a job during some of the hours the kids are
away. They estimate her income might be $300 per month.
Their monthly living expenses are as indicated in the sample
budget on page 57. Notice how certain expenses are
estimated to be lower if the husband is gone, while others,

---

*Social Security—One element that will reduce the income need is
social security. Assuming the federal government doesn't go into
bankruptcy, any wage earner who has been contributing to the social
security pool should have some benefits coming to his family in the
event of his death or disability. To find out what the payment would
be in your situation, contact your local Social Security office and ask
them to send you the information.

such as home maintenance, are estimated to rise. Certain
amounts are indicated to replace items that wear out, such as
the automobile and home furnishings. Income taxes are
obviously lower, and insurance premiums have dropped
significantly. Since the insurance and assets available on the
husband's death are adequate to carry the wife and children
as far as necessary, there is still no need for insurance on the
mother. However, if she had planned to completely support
the children after the death of her husband, some insurance
to replace her working income would be indicated to provide
for the children's continued support.

We've arrived at a monthly income necessary to support
the surviving spouse and children until the kids are grown.
After that the wife's needs will diminish, but this lowered
need will be offset by the loss of the social security payment.
The required income in our example is $1,450 per month,
and the amount needed after deducting her income ($300 per
month), and the estimated social security payment ($400 per
month), is approximately $750 per month, which must be
made up out of income from capital. Once we determine how
long that income needs to last, we can calculate how much
capital is necessary to provide it.

The typical approach taken by the insurance man is to
simply capitalize the income at the rate of interest that the
insurance company pays for policy proceeds left at interest.
For example, if the life insurance company pays 5% interest,
then the amount of capital required would be calculated
thusly: $750 times 12 months = $9,000 per year. Divide the
$9,000 by the 5% and you get $180,000. Thus $180,000, if
earning at the rate of 5%, would yield $9,000 per year.

The wife would then have a perpetual income of $9,000
per year and the capital would never be depleted. While this
is apparently true, the problem would surface next year. She
would have the $9,000 income, but she would find that next
year it would buy her significantly less than it will buy this
year. Her budget would suddenly jump by whatever the rate

of inflation happened to be. If it's 20% this year, next year she'll need to have $10,800 to buy the same goods and services. And so on every year thereafter.

Compensating for Inflation. Since there is no way to predict very far in advance what the rate of inflation may be, the calculation must integrate an unknown rate of inflation in order to determine what amount of capital is necessary to meet her income needs. The only way I can see that this can be done is to assume a rate of earnings that is variable but somehow constant in relation to inflation. Since interest rates tend to rise in inflating economies, I think the way to estimate need in this area is to assume that the surviving spouse will attempt to invest the assets in a way that will keep pace with both taxes and inflation. If inflation grew at 8% as it did in 1973 then she would have to have earned 8% (plus taxes) to break even for the year. If it runs at 20% in 1974, the same thing holds true. Now assuming she could do this, how much capital would she need? If her earnings were just equal to inflation and taxes, then it should be obvious that the income she consumes would have to come out of principal, and, therefore, the principal would be consumed. Many an investment advisor or stock salesman will tell you that you can do much better than this; that you'll be able to invest the money and not only meet inflation and taxes but make a profit as well. Think it over. Let's take 1974 as an example. According to the government figures the cost of living rose 12.2%. However, the things that your wife would have been spending money on, had she been in a widow's situation that year, might have increased much more. For example, food jumped almost 18%, and gasoline almost doubled. Clothes, automobiles, etc., likewise leaped at a pace that made 12.2% look like no inflation at all. So the fact is that her expenses might have gone up far more than the 12.2% overall average calculated by Uncle Sam.

Just for talking's sake, suppose her cost of living rose only

12.2%. Whatever she has her money invested in, other than tax-free municipal bonds, there's almost certain to be some tax to pay, but let's assume the lowest rate. Say that of her total income she pays only 10% out in state and federal taxes. She would need to be earning 12.2% to cover inflation, plus another 1.2% to cover the taxes on the income, meaning she would have to have her money growing at 13.4% per annum. And that was 1974! This year and next year what will inflation do? It will be much higher. And taxes too. So how would you rate your wife's chances of getting a safe 15% to 20% return on her invested capital? She's going to have to be both very astute and very fortunate to realize it year after year. It's a tough world in today's money markets.

The conclusion is that unless you consider your wife to be sharper than average when it comes to handling money, you'd better put away enough assets to last her for whatever number of years you want her to have an independent income, and cross your fingers that she'll get at least a zero true-rate-of-return.

In our example the couple decides that the wife should have this income until the children are through college, let's say until they're 23. That means another 15 years. Then she'll make a living on her own. Since the amount needed in today's dollars is $9,000 per year, that amount times the 15 years will equal $135,000. In other words, $135,000 will last the widow 15 years if it is invested at a rate of return that equals inflation and taxes, and she consumes it at the rate of $9,000 per year of today's dollars. The formula for determining the amount of capital required to meet the income needs of your dependents becomes simple: it is the amount per year in today's dollars times the number of years of support required. The only assumption you're making is they will be able to invest that capital at a rate that equals inflation plus taxes.

To finish the calculation of the amount of life insurance required, a couple of more steps are necessary. Total needs consist of the sum of the debts, an allowance for a home, a capital sum to provide income, money for final expenses and taxes, and perhaps a fund for the college education of the children.

The College Fund. In educational expenses we are again confronted with the problem of inflation. College costs have been rising at a rate even higher than general prices. The Life Insurance Institute annually publishes a list of all the colleges in the U.S. along with tuition costs and the cost of room and board.[24] In 1974-1975 the average cost of a state supported college or university, including room, board, and tuition for the year, is about $3,000. That's how much it is today, but how large a fund should be set up for a child whose college won't start until ten or twenty years in the future? The solution is to put away a lump sum equal to today's cost, and assume that the money will grow at a rate equal to the rate of inflation. It's possible to avoid paying taxes on the income the funds will be earning by putting them into a trust for the children. The income would be taxed to them rather than the widow, and since it's unlikely the children's income will be great enough to be taxed, the income to the fund will be tax free.

Whether or not to put money away for your children's education is a subjective decision on your part. Some parents feel they should provide the entire cost of four years of college, and graduate school as well, while others feel that partially assisting the children through the first four years is more than adequate. After you decide the amount you want to provide, add this amount to your total needs list.

In our example $177,500 is the total amount required to provide a comfortable living for our hypothetical family, at least through the college years of the children. If the widow were fortunate in the way the money was put to work, or in the amount she earned, or in keeping expenditures down, then the original capital would carry her much farther in life than the calculated 15 years.

Adding Back the Assets. The $177,500 of needs we've calculated in our example is not the amount of insurance necessary, for the present assets of the family will be owned by the wife on the death of the husband, and can be used to reduce the need. As a matter of fact, if the family at this point had $177,500 in assets there would be no reason to carry life insurance at all. Effectively they would be their own insurance company. The premiums that would have gone for insurance could be spent or invested for the future.

In our example, our family has assets amounting to $116,100 that would be available to the survivors. When subtracted from the total needs, this leaves them with a total life insurance requirement of $61,400.

After you have determined what your survivors' needs will be, make a list of the assets currently owned that can be used to satisfy these needs. To be realistic ask what any given asset would be able to be sold for if the breadwinner was not around. A doctor, for example, might value his practice, including accounts receivable, at $100,000. On his death, however, his widow might be hard pressed to collect those receivables, and might find it difficult to find another doctor to buy the equipment and good will. She could wind up selling the practice for half of what the doctor himself might have been able to get for it if alive.

Other assets should be carefully evaluated as well. Many limited partnership interests are non-liquid. If there is reasonable chance that they might turn out to be losers in the long run, they should be discounted when figuring the amount of capital available to meet her needs. Additionally, assets should be discounted by the income taxes that will be due on their liquidation. Income taxes due on the sale of an asset after the death of one of the owners will be partially determined by the way in which title is held. If for one reason or another you are holding title to property in a form

that doesn't avoid income taxes, then the tax liability should
be taken into consideration when your life insurance needs
are calculated.

LIFE INSURANCE NEEDS ESTIMATE

Capital Requirements

Debts	$ 8,500	
Income Taxes	1,000	
Probate and Estate Tax	2,000	
Final Expenses	3,000	
Education Fund	28,000	
Family Income	135,000	
Total Capital Requirements		$177,500

Available Assets

Stocks, Bonds	$ 17,000	
Income Real Estate (Equity)	23,000	
Coin Collection	14,000	
Second Car	2,100	
Husband's Business	60,000	
Total Available Assets		116,100
Total Life Insurance Needed		$ 61,400

Figure 16

Summary

In summary, the amount of life insurance you need is the
difference between the needs for capital of your surviving
dependents, and the total assets they'll have available. Once
you've established the size of the need, the next step is to
decide on the correct type of insurance.

PERMANENT OR TERM?
WILL THE REAL BARGAIN PLEASE STAND UP?

At this point you should know how much life insurance
you need, and on what members of the family. The next

question is what kind? There have been many exposés of the insurance industry, yet it continues year after year to sell hundreds of millions of dollars worth of the wrong kind of insurance to the gullible public. When you finish this chapter, I would hope you'll never again fall victim to the sophisticated deceit of any insurance company.

There are two ways that you can buy life insurance. You can buy pure death protection, or you can buy pure death protection that includes a savings account. The first is called *term* insurance, the other is called *cash value* insurance. Term is a word contrived by the insurance industry to have a negative impression on the prospect. It means either "in force for a limited term," or "terminating" depending on which agent you talk to. Insurance that falls in the cash value category is referred to as "permanent," and thereby is contrasted with terminating insurance. Tell me, would you rather have something that is permanent or terminating? Permanent seems so much more stable and secure. But is it?

TERM INSURANCE

Term insurance is sold as a simple wager with the insurance company. You want to cover the risk that you'll die this year. The insurance company is willing to make a wager with you that that event won't occur. They do it in much the same way that the casino in Las Vegas arranges the payoff on a bet on the roulette wheel. They make a wheel with 38 pockets in which the ball can fall. There is one chance in 38 that the ball will fall in any particular pocket. When you bet on one pocket, they will pay you only 36 to 1 if you win. Thus, if a one dollar bet were placed on each of the 38 pockets, the casino would make a net profit of $2 on each spin of the wheel.

So it is with an insurance company. They have mortality tables which are drawn from the number of people of any given age that die in any given year. These tables are expressed in number of deaths per thousand, and are periodically revised to reflect the increasing life expectancy of Americans. Figure 17 is a copy of the table that is currently being used by most insurance companies to calculate their rates. At age 35 this table predicts that 2.51 persons per thousand will die and that the remaining life expectancy of any 35 year old is 36.69 years. If every person in a group of 1,000 people went to the insurance company and asked to be insured for $1,000, the insurance company would know that it would probably have to pay claims totaling $2,510. In order to assure itself of a profit it would simply calculate its overhead costs for being in business, its commission costs for selling the policies, income taxes that would be due on its profits, and the profit it desired, and add them to the $2,510 it would have to pay out in claims, and divide the result up among the 1,000 applicants. In other words the policy should cost $2.51 per $1,000 worth of insurance plus the company's costs and profit.

The company goes one step further in assuring itself that it won't lose. It selects the best risks from among the applicants. It won't insure the 1,000 people at random and thus incur the 2.51 deaths that are the average. It will refuse to insure, or charge higher rates to anyone that shows a higher risk of dying by having some physical or moral handicap that places them in a higher risk category. Although I don't know how this affects the statistics, we might assume that if the 1,000 people represented by the mortality table only included people in good health, then the deaths per thousand might drop to 1.5 rather than the 2.51 who actually died. Thus the insurance company increases the odds even further in its favor. So if we look at the mortality table and estimate some expenses, commissions and profits, we might assume that for a reasonably healthy individual age 35 to buy $1,000 worth of insurance for one year he would probably have to pay around $2.00 to $3.00 per thousand. If you look at rate tables for one year term insurance at that age, you'll find the rates vary from about $2.50 to $5.00 per

TABLE OF MORTALITY

Age	Deaths Per 1,000	Expectation of Life	Age	Deaths Per 1,000	Expectation of Life
0	7.08	68.30	50	8.32	23.63
1	1.76	67.78	51	9.11	22.82
2	1.52	66.90	52	9.96	22.03
3	1.46	66.00	53	10.89	21.25
4	1.40	65.10	54	11.90	20.47
5	1.35	64.19	55	13.00	19.71
6	1.30	63.27	56	14.21	18.97
7	1.26	62.35	57	15.54	18.23
8	1.23	61.43	58	17.00	17.51
9	1.21	60.51	59	18.59	16.81
10	1.21	59.58	60	20.34	16.12
11	1.23	58.65	61	22.24	15.44
12	1.26	57.72	62	24.31	14.78
13	1.32	56.80	63	26.57	14.14
14	1.39	55.87	64	29.04	13.51
15	1.46	54.95	65	31.75	12.90
16	1.54	54.03	66	34.74	12.31
17	1.62	53.11	67	38.04	11.73
18	1.69	52.19	68	41.68	11.17
19	1.74	51.28	69	45.61	10.64
20	1.79	50.37	70	49.79	10.12
21	1.83	49.46	71	54.15	9.63
22	1.86	48.55	72	58.65	9.15
23	1.89	47.64	73	63.26	8.69
24	1.91	46.73	74	68.12	8.24
25	1.93	45.82	75	73.37	7.81
26	1.96	44.90	76	79.18	7.39
27	1.99	43.99	77	85.70	6.98
28	2.03	43.08	78	93.06	6.59
29	2.08	42.16	79	101.19	6.21
30	2.13	41.25	80	109.98	5.85
31	2.19	40.34	81	119.35	5.51
32	2.25	39.43	82	129.17	5.19
33	2.32	38.51	83	139.38	4.89
34	2.40	37.60	84	150.01	4.60
35	2.51	36.69	85	161.14	4.32
36	2.64	35.78	86	172.82	4.06
37	2.80	34.88	87	185.13	3.80
38	3.01	33.97	88	198.25	3.55
39	3.25	33.07	89	212.46	3.31
40	3.53	32.18	90	228.14	3.06
41	3.84	31.29	91	245.77	2.82
42	4.17	30.41	92	265.93	2.58
43	4.53	29.54	93	289.30	2.33
44	4.92	28.67	94	316.66	2.07
45	5.35	27.81	95	351.24	1.80
46	5.83	26.95	96	400.56	1.51
47	6.36	26.11	97	488.42	1.18
48	6.95	25.27	98	668.15	.83
49	7.60	24.45	99	1000.00	.50

Figure 17

thousand. If the only thing you need is insurance one year then pick the cheapest company and buy. Assuming that you may want to be insured for longer than one year, there are other considerations.

The Rate Goes Up Every Year. Notice I said the rate, not the premium. The rate is the cost per thousand dollars of insurance. The premium is the amount you pay the insurance company every year. One thing the mortality table makes clear is that more people die each year as age increases. If the insurance company is going to continue making a profit, they'll have to charge more each year for each $1,000 worth of insurance, and there's no way around it. To the person paying the premium this isn't always obvious, for frequently the premium for a policy will remain constant. There are two ways in which the insurance company can continue to profit while keeping your costs constant. One is to decrease the amount of insurance each year based on the increasing mortality risk. This is normally referred to as "decreasing" or "declining" term. A policy that starts at $10,000 and drops to zero over ten years in $1,000 increments is called ten-year decreasing term. If it declines to zero over twenty years it's called twenty-year decreasing term, and so on. Most companies that sell this type of insurance have policies that decline over 10, 15, 20, 25, 30, and 40 years and some companies offer decreasing term to age 65 or age 100. When the agent shows you the cost per thousand on these policies you'll notice that the cost goes up as the length of the decline increases. This is your cost for the right to be guaranteed you can buy insurance in those future years.

Decreasing term insurance is logical for a number of needs: for example, if you have an installment debt and the amount of the debt is decreasing each year, you can buy a policy that will decline along with the debt. Mortgage insurance is nothing but decreasing term insurance, but since it's often sold by the lender and goes under the fancy name of mortgage insurance you'll usually find it more expensive than the same product bought under the name of decreasing term (just like buying the generic name vs. the trade name in drugs).

Many investment salesmen recommend decreasing term on the assumption that your insurance need will go down every year as your investments increase in value. Look carefully at this concept and the figures involved. Even though your assets seem to be increasing every year, the rising costs of living may offset them and you may need more insurance rather than less.

I previously stated there were ways that the insurance company could keep your premium level while increasing the cost-per-thousand of your insurance. The first was to decrease the amount of insurance, the second is to make you prepay the increasing costs in the early years of the policy. This is called level term insurance, and goes under the names of 5-year renewable term, 10-year renewable term, term to age 65, etc. It's a level amount of death benefit and a level premium. In the case of 5-year renewable term, the company keeps your premium level for five years then jumps it to a new five year level. As opposed to annual renewable term in which the premium jumps up every year, the company will take the average premium over the five years and charge you that from the beginning. You're paying more the first two years than the term rate should be, and less the last two years, and thus the rate seems to be level. In term to age 65, the premiums are level from the date you take out the policy up to age 65.

Buying insurance where the premium is leveled over long periods just doesn't make good sense. In the end you're going to pay an increasing cost-per-thousand every year due to increasing mortality, so why pay in advance just to keep the premium level? You're just letting them use your money at no interest.

Rates for term will vary from company to company, and usually the companies with the biggest advertising budgets are the most expensive (as they prefer not to sell term at all).

After you've decided what type of term insurance you want, get a variety of price quotes from companies. If you want some assistance in this task get hold of Consumer Union's *Guide to Life Insurance.*[25] Reprinted from the January, February and March 1974 issues of *Consumer Reports*, it contains a wealth of premium comparisons that should enable you to select the lowest cost company.

CASH VALUE INSURANCE

Suppose you decide to begin to save money on a regular investment plan. You have $100 per month that you're willing to put away regularly and you want a good deal of safety. So you walk down to your friendly savings and loan and talk with the new accounts man. The conversation goes something like this:

"Hi," you say, "my wife and I were thinking of opening a savings account and we'd like to deposit $100 per month toward our retirement."

"Oh, great," says he, "I have just the account for you. It offers security and growth. If you promise to put away $100 a month for thirty years you'll have . . ." glances down at a chart, "$54,000 when you reach age 65, that's thirty years from now. Not bad, right?"

"Great," you reply, glancing at your wife "it really adds up, doesn't it?"

"It certainly does. Furthermore, if you want to borrow money from us any time along the way, we'll loan you up to the amount in your account for only 6% interest. Now where else can you borrow money for only 6%?"

"You mean you'll *loan me my own money* and I pay you 6%?"

"Well, of course you continue to earn interest on the money as though it were still in your account, so the net cost to you is only 3%," he smiles somewhat uneasily.

"By the way" you ask, "the account amounts to $54,000 at the end of the thirty years. What compound rate of interest is that?"

The banker fidgets. "2½% per year, but I must point out that it's tax deferred until you actually draw it out, so that's not bad considering how high taxes are nowadays."

"Well, it doesn't sound too good to me," you reply, "but I guess maybe we'll start out and we can always move the account if we find a better rate somewhere else."

"Well, I must point out," he replies, "that our costs and overhead are such that if you wanted to close out your account at the end of the first year, we would have to keep the amount you've deposited to cover our expenses. However, if you didn't close out until the end of the second year then we'd give you back $600."

"But I would have deposited $2400 by that time."

"Well, we have expenses, you know!"

"Let me get this straight," your wife chimes in, "we open a savings account, you pay us 2½% interest, nothing is credited to our account for the first year and half, and after that if we want to use our money you'll loan it to us for 6%?"

"Well, don't forget the tax feature, and also other advantages I've failed to mention, like the fact that since you lose your first eighteen month's deposits, this tends to force you to continue to make regular deposits. A kind of forced savings plan."

"Any other 'benefits?' " she asks skeptically.

"Well yes, one more. We offer you a chance to buy decreasing-term life insurance at the same rates you could buy it outside. In fact, I should have mentioned that we require that you buy some proportionate to the amount of your savings. We have several different plans to offer."

By this time you have your coat in hand and you both rise and bid the "banker" adieu. Thanks, but no thanks, you snicker. You're too smart for this con artist; after all there are much better deals for saving your money at a dozen other banks, savings and loans, and thrift institutions within walking distance. What does he take you for, sucker of the week?

Are you really that smart? Do you now own any whole life, retirement income, or endowment life insurance policies? In other words have you ever bought cash value life insurance? Then you've already deposited money with this banker, and probably on worse terms than outlined above. He didn't come at you honestly and tell you what his real product was when he sold it to you. He told you you were buying permanent insurance and he was going to help you build a living estate as well as provide for your family in the event of your death. Life insurance companies in the United States have caused people to deposit over $200 billion under terms just as bad or worse than those outlined above, and not one policyholder in a hundred will ever know what is really happening.

The life insurance industry didn't build those massive monuments of concrete, steel and glass from the profits of selling insurance. They built them from the profits realized by borrowing money from a gullible public at 1, 2 and 3% a year interest, and lending it back to the public in the form of mortgages on homes and office buildings at a rate of 6, 8, 10 and 12%. They are in the finance business, and insurance is merely a front.

So that you can inbed this fact clearly in your mind, without a chance of ever being brainwashed again by another well-intentioned insurance agent, let's go through and analyze a typical cash-value policy. Rather than take the most expensive policies on the market, such as those of the bigger more advertised companies like John Hancock, Mutual of New York, or Prudential, I'll take an actual policy of one of the less expensive non-participating companies. The following is an illustration of a policy sold by a company that is considered to be one of the best and least expensive companies on the market. It is a whole life policy sold to a man age 35, and is for an amount of $100,000. The rate-per-thousand of face amount is $16.93 and in addition there is an annual policy fee of $15.00 regardless of the size of the policy. The premium comes to $1,708 per year. Each year the company credits a certain amount to the cash value of the policy. The cash value table is shown in Figure 18. In other words, if the premium is paid every year until age 65, the policy can be dropped and the owner will receive $54,400 in cash. Since he will have paid in only $51,240, any good insurance agent will tell you that he has had $100,000 worth of insurance for 30 years for free, and made a profit of $3,160 to boot.

What Figure 18 points up is that the insurance company is not providing the insured with $100,000 worth of insurance during the term of the contract. The insurance benefit is decreasing every year by the amount of the cash value increase. Since the cash value always belongs to the policy owner, the insurance agent can't claim that it constitutes part of the "insurance".

In fact, the policy offers almost exactly the same amount of insurance as a decreasing-term-to-age-100 would offer. Suppose I went to the same insurance company and wanted to buy the same amount of term insurance each year that was actually provided under the death benefit of the Whole Life policy. The difference between the cost of the term and the cost of the whole life policy could be invested. Assuming a compound interest rate of 3% on the invested savings, you would accumulate $55,285 in your savings account at the end of 30 years. That's $885 more than you'd have in cash value in your policy. In other words, whole life is almost exactly the same as taking out a declining term policy and investing the difference at 3%. The cash value table also illustrates an earlier point: that you are paying a higher rate-per-thousand for insurance every year, whether your insurance agent will admit it or not. You're paying a level premium, the death benefit is going down, and the amount of savings you have on deposit is going up.

Cash value life insurance is simply a disguised form of term plus savings. What about the other types of cash value

CASH VALUE TABLE — WHOLE LIFE
MALE AGE 35 — $100,000
Annual Premium = $1708

End of Policy Year	Cash Value	+	Insurance	=	Death Benefit
1	$ 200		$99,800		$100,000
2	1,900		98,100		100,000
3	3,600		96,400		100,000
4	5,300		94,700		100,000
5	7,100		92,900		100,000
6	8,900		91,100		100,000
7	10,700		89,300		100,000
8	12,600		87,400		100,000
9	14,500		85,500		100,000
10	16,400		83,600		100,000
11	18,400		81,600		100,000
12	20,300		79,700		100,000
13	22,400		77,600		100,000
14	14,400		75,600		100,000
15	26,500		73,500		100,000
16	38,600		71,400		100,000
17	30,700		69,300		100,000
18	32,900		67,100		100,000
19	35,100		64,900		100,000
20	37,300		62,700		100,000
21	39,300		60,700		100,000
22	41,100		58,900		100,000
23	42,800		57,200		100,000
24	44,400		55,600		100,000
25	46,000		54,000		100,000
26	47,700		52,300		100,000
27	49,400		50,600		100,000
28	51,100		48,900		100,000
29	52,800		47,200		100,000
30	54,400		45,600		100,000

Figure 18

insurance? Like endowment, 20-pay life, or retirement income, for example. The only difference between these forms of insurance is the amount of premium that goes toward savings every year. If the ratio between the cost of the term insurance and the savings portion of the premium changes, the name of the policy changes. For example, endowment at age 65 means that at age 65 there is cash value in the policy equal to the face value of the policy. If you have a $10,000 endowment policy it will have $10,000 in cash value on the day it endows. To accomplish this you'll simply pay a higher premium each year, with more of your dollars going into savings and less into insurance. In an endowment policy the amount of insurance purchased declines rapidly to the date of the endowment. A whole life policy could be said to be an endowmnent policy that endows at approximately age 100.

Figure 19 gives you a rough illustration of three types of insurance a 35-year-old could buy, and the rates of decline of insurance protection versus cash value. No matter how you buy it, however, the cost of the pure insurance protection still declines, still costs more every year, and would still be replaceable by a simple term policy, leaving the opportunity to invest the difference at a rate hopefully higher than the 3% the insurance company offers.

If it is true that the insurance company is really a financing institution, and that cash value insurance is just term with a savings account, is there any reason why a person would want to buy cash-value insurance? Why don't the life insurance agents sell term instead? There are only two reasons a person would want to buy cash-value insurance. First, if they need some type of policemen hovering over them to force them to save, this is one way to do it. The policyholder should know that he can borrow that cash value out of the policy at any time; thus, his forced savings is really not forced. The cost for this discipline is so enormous and the psychology so ridiculous that it can hardly be considered a rational reason

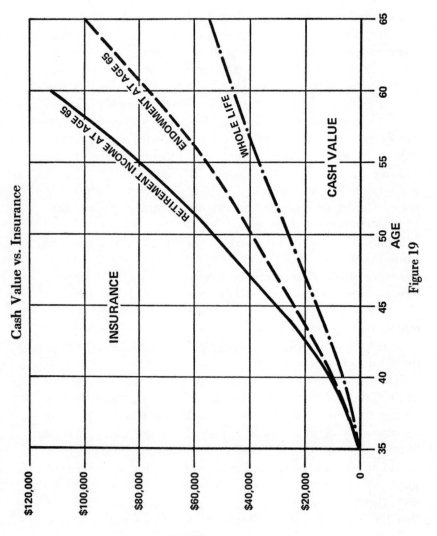

Cash Value vs. Insurance

Figure 19

for buying whole life. The second reason that a person might buy cash-value insurance is if the tax advantages make it effectively cheaper than term.

Minimum Deposit Insurance. This can sometimes be done through what is known in the trade as *minimum deposit* insurance. Minimum deposit simply means that you buy regular cash value insurance, but every year you take out a maximum loan against the cash value of the policy. Thus no cash value builds up and you have the money to invest that would normally be sitting with the insurance company. The company pays you 3% interest on the savings portion of your policy. If you borrow against the policy the mechanics are something like borrowing against a savings account at the bank, wherein you use your savings passbook as collateral, and get a favorable rate of interest on the loan. The banker, knowing that you have $1,000 on deposit in a savings account will loan you $1,000 and charge you something like 2 or 3% over what he is paying you on the savings account. He has no risk, and earns the spread between what he pays you and what you pay him. There may be reasons why a person might at some time want to do this. For example, you have a time deposit and if you drew the money out early you'd have an interest penalty. Usually it doesn't make sense. In a life insurance policy, however, it sometimes does make sense. The life insurance company treats a loan in the same way the banker does. They leave your savings untouched, still earning the magnificent 3% interest. But interest on the loan is charged to you at the rate of 6%. Thus they make the 3% difference as profit. They don't like to do this and you'll be constantly encouraged to repay the loan and bring your policy back up to "full death benefit," inasmuch as the loan reduces the amount that the company would pay your beneficiary in the event of your death. Why don't they want to make that 3% profit? Because if they lend your money to anyone else they can make two or three times as much profit.

Now comes the tax advantage to you. The company charges you 6% interest and this is deductible on your tax return as an interest expense. If you are in the happy state of being in a 50% tax bracket you'll save half the interest. In other words, the net amount that you'll be paying to the insurance company for the use of the money is 3%. Since they are paying you 3% and under current tax laws that amount *is not being taxed to you as income,* you are in a break-even situation. You have the cash value out of the policy and you can invest it and all you have left is the term insurance portion of the contract. You have effectively separated the cash value insurance into its two components, and eliminated the savings element.

What's the advantage to this? Life insurance companies heavily load their term policies in order to make them profitable. Since profit from their cash value products is realized from the use of the cash values, the term portion of these policies is less expensive than it would be if purchased separately. If you minimum deposit a cash-value policy, you may find the net cost substantially less than a similar term policy.

Qualifying for the Tax Deduction. The IRS says that interest paid on a policy loan is not deductible if the insurance was bought under a plan of borrowing. They call it a plan of borrowing if the policy owner borrows more than the amount of three full premiums out of the first seven years of the policy. Anyone wishing to minimum deposit a policy must be careful to pay in full four of the first seven years and not borrow more than the amount of the premium from the other three. After seven years he can strip the policy every year. You can lose that interest deduction if you don't pay the interest in full and in cash. Simply using a loan from the policy to pay the interest is not enough; write a separate check for the interest.

High tax bracket policyholders should look carefully at old cash value policies before deciding to drop them for term. It might be possible to minimum deposit them and wind up with a cost less than a new term policy.

Why You Can't Get the Truth. Why don't insurance agents tell the client the truth about cash value insurance? Either they don't know, or they find it so profitable to sell cash value insurance that they don't want to know. On the $100,000 policy discussed earlier, the agent will earn a commission of $1110.20 or 65% of the first year premium. Every year thereafter that the policy remains in force he'll earn 5% or $85.40. In addition, the general agent he works for (he may very well be the general agent himself) will earn half the agent's commission the first year (32.5% or $555.10), and 7% of the premium each year thereafter ($119.56). Between the two of them they will earn 97.5% of the first year premium, or $1,665.30, and 12% each year thereafter, or $205.00. Pretty profitable, right? And what if the agent had sold you an annual renewable term policy for $100,000? The premium would have been $290 and his commission only 40%, or $116.00, and the second year 10%, or $29.00. The general agent again would get an amount equal to half the agent's commission, or $58.00, and 7% the second year. Do you think that this commission structure would have any bearing on what type of insurance that agent is going to present? In one case, he and his general agent make a commission of $1,665 with renewals of $205 per year thereafter, and in the other case, they make $283 with renewals of $49.30. They make six times the profit selling one over the other. Is it any wonder that most of the insurance in force is cash value insurance?

Are the agents dishonest? Not at all. Many agents do sell term. Many of those who push cash-value insurance simply don't know the facts themselves. They have been literally brainwashed by the insurance companies to believe that cash value is the greatest thing since the wheel. I constantly meet agents who have enormous amounts of cash-value insurance on their own lives. The idiocy of it boggles the mind. When confronted with the truth they put on blinders and turn up the background noise, for the truth is an absolute threat to their entire careers and their self-esteem. They must either admit you're right and stop selling cash-value insurance (thus cutting their income to one sixth of what it formerly was), or knowingly con their clients. Instead of doing either, they just refuse to listen.

MUTUAL VS. STOCK COMPANIES

There are two types of companies or policies that can be purchased in life insurance. One that pays dividends or one that doesn't. One is called *participating* and the other *non-participating*, or par and non-par for short. A mutual company sells participating contracts. Non-participating contracts are sold by stock companies. Stock companies are owned by stockholders who share in the profits of the company, while the mutual companies are supposedly owned by the policyholders, in a kind of cooperative.

The advertising of the mutual companies would lead you to believe that your costs will be far less due to the fact that the mutual company will let you participate in the profits of the company through dividends. They do pay dividends; however, these are not part of the profits of the company, as they would lead you to believe. They simply charge a higher premium for the same type of policy than does the average stock company and later on refund you the overcharge in the form of a dividend. Since they hold this overcharge for some years before returning it, you lose the use of this money. The company, in that it ostensibly is not seeking to profit from your business, is run like any non-profit organization. Extremely high overhead, high reserves and low efficiency eat up any savings that you might have realized.

If there is any doubt that a dividend is not really part of the profits of the company, check with the IRS. They state that dividends on insurance policies are not taxable inasmuch as they constitute a refund of overpayment of premium. In general, buy non-participating, non-dividend-paying insurance. It'll save you money in the short run, and the long run.

How to Choose a Company

The way to buy life insurance is to buy the cheapest you can find that meets your needs. In most states insurance laws are strict enough to prevent insurance companies from selling insurance if they are not financially capable of meeting claims, Equity Funding notwithstanding. The odds against your buying from a company that might go defunct are minimal. Assuming you're only buying term, they'd have to go under at the same time you die, which would compound the odds in your favor. You should be buying by net cost alone, and the only way I can suggest that you approach this problem is as follows:

1. Determine the amount of insurance you need before contacting any agents.

2. Determine the length of time during which you'll need to carry the insurance.

3. From the above, determine which you think might be the best form of insurance to buy; that is, level term, declining term, or minimum deposit.

4. Call several independent insurance agents and tell them what you're looking for. Make it *clear* to them that you're knowledgeable and you're shopping the market to find the lowest cost policies.

5. Compare the rates that are submitted to you.

If agents know you're shopping and they fear being underbid, they'll go to their rate books and try to find a term rate that will beat out the competition. Don't hesitate to tell them the rate that the competition has quoted. That will force them to find a cheaper company. The first companies they select will be the companies that offer the highest commissions. They'll only look at the other companies if they're sure that they are going to lose the business. After all, a small commission is better than none.

Riders

Insurance agents will recommend a variety of riders that can be added at extra premium to a life insurance policy. The most common are accidental death benefit, waiver of premium, and insurability options. First of all, there is usually no reason to buy an accidental death benefit. If you need insurance you should buy enough to cover your need no matter what the cause of death. Any extra premium that would be paid for accidental death would create surplus coverage in excess of your true needs. Don't ever buy insurance you don't need; it's a very bad gamble. If you want to gamble, you'd be farther ahead to play the extra premium at the crap table in Las Vegas.

Waiver of premium is actually disability income insurance. You are buying enough income in the case of disability to pay your life insurance premiums. Generally I recommend that this rider be added except in the case of minimum deposit or cash value insurance, since in that case the person would have to buy disability income insurance on the cash value portion of the policy, too. It would be better to use those premium dollars to buy regular disability insurance, because the provisions of the waiver of premium clause in a life insurance policy are generally not as good as the provisions of a disability contract from one of the better disability companies. That subject will be covered in detail later in this chapter.

As far as the future insurability option is concerned, if you are certain you will be needing more insurance in the future, but you don't want to take it out now, then it may be a reasonable thing for you to buy.

Just remember that the riders added on to a policy are

some of the most profitable things an insurance company can sell, so buy them only if you're certain you need them.

BUSINESS INSURANCE

So far I've been discussing life insurance from the standpoint of an individual purchasing a policy for himself. A great deal of the life insurance sold today is sold to businesses or individuals through businesses. The life insurance industry uses business as an inroad to sell cash-value life insurance in quantities individuals would never buy. Business life insurance falls into three major categories: Pension plan insurance, group term and buy-sell insurance. Pension insurance is discussed in Chapter V.

Group Insurance

Under current IRS regulations any corporation is allowed to purchase up to $50,000 worth of group-term life insurance on an employee and deduct the premium as a business expense without the premium being charged to the employee as taxable income. This is currently the only way that the cost of life insurance can directly become a deductible expense. In many circumstances this can result in a much lower net cost than any other method of purchasing insurance, and is most effective in a situation where there are only one or two full-time employees; for example, a professional corporation where there is only a doctor, or a doctor and a nurse.

One of the confusing elements of group term insurance deals with how much insurance is required to be carried on the other employees of a corporation in relation to what is carried by the top men. This ratio is determined by the laws of the state in which the insurance company is domiciled, rather than the laws of the state in which the policy is sold, with the result that different companies will have different requirements for employee participation in the plan. Many companies purposely register their group policies in states favorable to this problem. In Delaware, for example, the rules state that for corporations with under ten employees, all full-time employees must be covered and the ratio of coverage can be either a uniform percentage of salary or a fixed amount of insurance for each salary bracket. In the latter case the employees are grouped arbitrarily into classes such as officers, supervisors, and all other employees. No bracket can exceed 2½ times the next lower bracket, and the lowest bracket must be at least 10% of the highest bracket. Since there is no requirement that there be any employees in any of the brackets, an employer could and would probably wind up insuring his full time employees for 10% of what he insured himself for. The doctor who took $50,000 worth of insurance would insure his employee for $5,000 under this method. The whole procedure is simple, and the time required to make the calculations minimal in relation to the potential premium savings available.

Life insurance companies, ever trying to find ways to sell cash value insurance, have come up with what is called *group ordinary,* a method of selling cash value insurance in place of group term. They simply substitute an ordinary life policy for the group term, and the corporation pays for and deducts the premium for the term portion of the policy while the employee pays the cash value portion. Any way it's examined it's nothing more than a regular cash value insurance policy, and the comparison should be made as to whether it is cheaper to buy the group term or minimum deposit the group ordinary. It all depends on the cost of the particular policy and the tax bracket of the employee.

Buy-Sell Insurance

In professional corporations the law requires that provisions be made to retire the stock of any shareholder that dies, becomes disabled, or leaves the corporation. Additionally, the corporation will normally suffer some financial strain from the loss of a producing shareholder due to the continuing overhead burden.

In cases of death or disability, the corporation has the option of covering its financial risk through either insurance, or by having the remaining shareholders pay their pro-rata share of the losses personally. In order to determine when insurance should be used, and in what amounts, consideration should be given to the interests of the remaining shareholders, as well as the one who dies or is disabled.

The decedent shareholder will want his estate to realize the full value of his corporate stock including both corporate assets and receivables. Whether the value of these assets passes to his estate in an immediate lump sum payment, or in a series of payments over two or three years is normally not critical. Personal life insurance policies should cover the immediate needs of his beneficiaries.

The surviving shareholders are liable for redemption of the decedents stock at its agreed upon value. By arranging to pay out the value of assets over an extended period of time, and to pay out the receivables either as collected, or over an extended period of time, there is a negligible financial burden of the remaining shareholders. The fixed assets are normally low, and the collection of receivables offsets the payment. Also, the assets become the property of the remaining shareholders, and can be resold to a new shareholder. In either case, there is no net loss.

There can be, however, a substantial overhead burden that may continue until a replacement can be found for the decedent. Assuming the decedent's share of the overhead could be reduced by 10 or 20% and that a replacement could be found and be on the job within six months, then the potential loss to the remaining shareholders could be defined as 80% of six months' overhead.

From the decedent's point of view, life insurance contracts funding the liabilities of overhead, assets, and receivables are

not a good investment. He has paid his share of the premiums
up until his death, but his estate does not benefit. It receives
only the value of his shares of stock, which it would have
gotten even without the life insurance. From the point of
view of the remaining shareholders, however, the financial
burden of the decedents death could be absorbed by life
insurance proceeds. Insurance to fund the death risk in a
corporate stock redemption plan is protection for the
surviving shareholders, and is of no value to the decedent.
Since the only risk of loss is in the overhead burden, this is
the only risk that calls for insurance.

Summary

If you haven't yet reached financial independence, and
others are dependent on you for support, you probably need
life insurance. Recognize that life insurance companies are
your friendly adversaries. They and their agents can't be
trusted to calculate your true needs, tell you who in your
family should be insured, or recommend the correct type of
insurance. You must be your own informed counsel in this
area.

After reading this chapter, you should have a good
understanding of the types of products available to you. Buy
only term or minimum deposit, buy from a non-par
company, and skip the fancy riders. Be careful not to
over-insure when you calculate your needs, and review your
coverage every two years. The money you save is yours to
keep.

DISABILITY INSURANCE

Throughout the discussion on insurance I have emphasized
that you only insure a potential economic loss that would
seriously affect your standard of living or your program for
accumulating wealth. The most significant loss that any
producing person can suffer would be the loss of the ability

to earn. Yet this is one loss that is seldom properly covered by insurance. Only in the last few years have disability income insurance policies been widely sold, and their sale is still limited primarily to the highly-paid professional market.

How many people who own a $50,000 home fail to cover it with fire insurance? Not very many. And rightly so, as a $50,000 loss would be a serious setback to most people. Contrast that loss with the loss a 35-year-old earning $25,000 per year would suffer if disabled. He would have lost $750,000 by age 65! A loss few could stand.

What are the chances of becoming disabled? According to the 1964 Commissioners Disability Table, 50.3% of all men now aged 35 will suffer a disability lasting at least 90 days prior to age 65. One in ten will suffer permanent disability. The chances of suffering a disabling sickness or injury are substantially greater than the chances of dying during any time period.

If you don't carry disability income insurance, carefully review this chapter to see if you should. If you have it, review your coverage after reading this chapter to see if you have the right kind, the right amount, and the lowest premium. It's probably the most important insurance you carry.

How Much Should You Carry?

The amount of insurance you carry is not related to your income, but to your monthly living expenses. The budget sheet on page 57 is your first tool in determining the size of your need. Column three lists your expenses as they would be in the event of disability. From this figure you could subtract the amount of any coverage you might have under Workmen's Compensation, State Disability Income Insurance, salary continuation plans from your employer, or Social Security. If you don't already know the amounts of benefits you would receive from these sources, contact your local agency office and inquire.

The other two sources, outside charity, that you'd have

available to meet your expenses in the event of disability
would be your accumulated assets and individual disability
income insurance. By adding up your total assets and
subtracting your total liabilities you'll arrive at your net
worth. Dividing this figure by the annual income needed to
live, will give you the number of years you'll be able to
survive without income. Unless that number of years substantially exceeds your life expectancy, you'd be wise to
conserve those assets for later, covering your immediate
needs with insurance and keeping the nest-egg for later years
when the insurance runs out or becomes worthless due to
inflation.

Policy Variables

There are three variables to any disability income policy.
First is the amount of the benefit during periods of disability,
second is the length of time for which the benefit will be
paid, and third is the waiting period after disability starts and
before the benefits begin. Disabilities are categorized as either
accident caused or sickness caused, and waiting periods and
benefit periods can be different for the two. Your premium
will depend on the structure of the benefits you choose.

Disability Vs. Inflation

By mid-1974 prices were rising at 12% per year. If your
current living expenses are $2,000 per month and prices
continue to rise at that rate, in ten years your expenses will
be $6,300 per month, in twenty years $19,000 per month,
and in thirty years a staggering $60,000 per month!!

Don't panic. If you continue to work, your income should
rise proportionately. However, a problem will arise if you
become disabled. If you're relying on disability insurance to
meet your needs, you may find that what would pay all your
expenses comfortably today, won't pay for your groceries ten
years from now. Even policies that offer cost-of-living

escalators limit the increase to 3% to 5% per year and charge an extra premium for that benefit. If the present rate of inflation continues or increases, 3% to 5% won't help much.

How can you cope with the financial effects of a long term disability in an inflating economy? With great difficulty. Figure 20 shows roughly what one dollar of premium will buy in annual disability benefits (30 day wait) from a typical company for three standard benefit periods, and what the purchasing power of the total benefit would be at two levels of inflation.

AGE	BENEFIT PERIOD	ANNUAL BENEFIT	TOTAL BENEFIT	Purchasing Power of Total Benefits In Todays Dollars	
				8% Inflation	12% Inflation
30	5 Years	$52	$ 260	$208	$187
	35 Years (age 65)	$35	$1,225	$408	$286
	45 Years (life)	$31	$1,395	$375	$255
40	5 Years	$35	$ 175	$139	$126
	25 Years (age 65)	$25	$ 625	$266	$196
	35 Years (life)	$21	$ 735	$250	$172

WHAT $1 OF PREMIUM WILL BUY

Figure 20

The important conclusions that should be reached from looking at these figures are: 1. On long term coverage the purchasing power of total benefits could be cut down to one-fourth or one-fifth by inflation. 2. You wind up with more total purchasing power by buying an *Age 65 Benefit* than by spending the same premium dollar to buy a *Lifetime Benefit*.

There is no way you can be sure that the benefit you buy, no matter how large, will not be outdistanced by inflation. One way to partially secure yourself against this risk is by not buying any long-term benefits, but rather by buying very large short-term benefits. Suppose you're 40 now, your living expenses are $2,000 per month and you want to have enough money to meet them until age 65, but you don't know how high prices will go. Since $2,000 times 12 months times 25 years equals $600,000 you'll need a $600,000 benefit, but in today's dollars. You might solve this by buying $10,000 per month of coverage for a five year benefit period. The total amount you'd collect would be $10,000 times 60 months or $600,000. The purchasing power of the $600,000 would be somewhat eroded even in the short period of five years, but it would be much better than collecting the same amount over 25 years. Since you would be collecting high benefits even for short term disabilities, and there are many more short term disabilities than long term, the premium will be much higher in buying your total benefit in the first five years of disability.

In summary, when you determine how much coverage you want, don't rely on the disability salesman. Figure out your budget, tally your assets and liabilities, and compensate for inflation. When the salesman says you can help offset inflation by purchasing future insurability options (the right to buy more insurance in the future), remember this isn't going to help solve the problem unless the option gives you the right to buy the additional insurance even when you are disabled and collecting benefits. Don't buy benefits more than fifteen years in the future if you can help it. Remember, paying extra for a lifetime benefit as opposed to an age 65 benefit is a waste of money if that income will be received 30 years in the future, when dollars will have depreciated. You'd be better off to save the difference and invest it.

Types of Policies

There are two types of policies available. First is a non-cancellable, guaranteed renewable policy issued to an individual. It is, as the name suggests, not cancellable by the company as long as premiums are paid on time, and guaranteed to be renewable to some future age such as age 65 or for life. The second type of policy is a group policy which covers members of a group or association (usually on a voluntary basis). Typically, group policies are renewable to group members at the option of the insurance company, and rates are subject to change by the company.

Disability companies believe that if they insure an individual for too great a benefit he may decide that it is more profitable to become disabled than to continue working. Consequently those companies that offer individual policies will only issue between 40% and 60% of a person's regular earned income. The higher a person's income the lower the percentage the insurance company will cover, and in addition they usually set an absolute upper limit of around $3,500 per month regardless of the income of the insured. These limits are both issue and participation limits, so the insurance an applicant already has in force is considered when determining the upper maximum. If your income qualifies you for $3,000 per month of coverage, and you already carry $1,500, an individual non-can carrier will only issue another $1,500. Group carriers don't operate according to the same rules. If you belong to an association that is covered by a group carrier and apply for group coverage, they normally won't inquire about your current coverage. They'll issue according to their maximum limits regardless of how much other insurance you're carrying. Thus, if you want to insure for more than the maximum limit that a non-can carrier will issue, first buy his maximum and after it is issued and in force, apply to your group carrier for the maximum they will issue. Once the policy is in force with the non-can carrier it can't be cancelled.

Another method of buying a larger amount of coverage is through a buy-sell policy. If you are in business with partners, some companies have come out with policies which will buy out a disabled partner's share of the business by paying disability benefits up to the amount of the partner's interest in the business. Usually these policies have a one year waiting period, and benefit periods of between two and five years. They can be issued in excess of any individual policies carried by the participants, and frequently carry a reduced premium over the cost of a regular non-can policy with the same benefits.

Dual Benefit Periods

Should accident and sickness caused disabilities have different benefit periods? I can't imagine why. It's strange to find individuals with policies that have lifetime accident benefits, but only two to five year sickness benefits. If you're totally disabled, why would the way in which it happened have any effect on the length of time that you'll need to have income? Long term accident benefits are usually sold on the basis that they're so cheap, why not have them? Statistically anyone over age 35 is far more likely to suffer a long term disability from sickness than from accident. Accidents usually result in quick recuperation or death, and that's why they're cheaper.

Waiting Periods

How long should your waiting period be? How long can you go without income before you begin to suffer serious financial problems that affect your standard of living or your wealth accumulation goals? Since the key to savings is to be your own insurance company whenever possible, you should have as long a waiting period as possible before the benefits start, thus reducing your premium. The insurance companies lower the premium as the waiting period lengthens, but unfortunately they load the basic policy so that you don't save as much in premium as the reduced risk would seem to warrant. For a forty-year-old male professional a $1,000 per month benefit (to age 65) with a ninety-day waiting period would cost about $388 per year. The same benefit with a thirty day wait would cost $492 per year. Thus for an extra $104 per year you would be paid an extra two months benefit in the event of a prolonged disability. This would mean if you were disabled for 90 days you would receive $2,000 that you wouldn't have otherwise received and the total cost was $104. If you had a ninety day disability only once in the first 19 years of the policy you would collect enough to pay the extra premium (discounted for 12% inflation it would be 11 years). You must realize that the insurance company has already calculated the odds against that disability occurring, and the odds are against you collecting on the bet. So even if it seems cheap to buy that extra coverage, don't buy it unless it's needed.

Selecting the Policy

Once you have decided how much you need, how long a benefit period you need, and how long a waiting period you can handle, select the least expensive policy that provides the best contract. Unlike life insurance, the wording of disability income insurance contracts is not as fixed by law. Contracts vary and every clause must be carefully reviewed and compared against other available contracts before a selection can be made. The only way to do it is to read the contracts thoroughly yourself. Don't rely on an agent who works for one of the companies. Although there may be as many as fifty contractual points that must be compared, here are the more important ones.

1. **Definition of Disability.** When is the insured considered totally disabled? First, is it when he can't perform his regular occupation or when he can't perform *any* type of work for pay? Second, does this definition change after a short period

of time? For example, one contract says that the insured is
"considered totally disabled when he is unable to perform
the duties of any gainful occupation for which he is
reasonably fitted having due regard for his age, education and
experience." While another says the insured is totally
disabled "when completely unable to engage in his regular
occupation: however, after Monthly Indemnity has been
payable to the insured's 55th birthday or for sixty months,
whichever is longer, the insured is totally disabled when
unable to engage in *any* gainful occupation for which he is
reasonably fitted by education, training or experience, giving
due consideration to his economic status at the beginning of
disability."

The first contract will only pay benefits if the insured is so
completely disabled that he can't do anything for a living. A
physician, insured under this type of contract, could lose an
arm and an eye, but still be able to function as a clerk in a
grocery store so he wouldn't be able to collect payments.
Under the second example a surgeon would be paid if unable
to act as a surgeon even though he might be able to perform
as a general practitioner.

Most contracts redefine disability at some point in time. If
a person is being paid benefits under a lifetime benefit
provision and reaches age 55 (or collects for 60 months) this
contract would require that his ability to earn be reassessed
and for example, if a surgeon were able to become a teacher
or a general practitioner, then at that point he would no
longer be considered totally disabled. Provided, of course,
that the income from his new occupation was reasonably
commensurate with his prior income.

Disability income insurance contracts have changed considerably in the last few years; as competition increases and
the product becomes more widely used it's likely that better
and better contracts will be offered. Five years ago sickness
benefits to age 65 were the longest offered and a person
could only be insured in his specialty or occupation for a

maximum of five years before the definition of total disability changed to force him into any occupation. Today the better companies all offer lifetime sickness benefits (at least for disabilities occurring prior to age 50) and total disability is considered by most companies to mean inability to perform your regular occupation until age 65 or for at least ten years.

The definition of total disability is probably the most important part of a disability contract. Read it carefully and compare it with the other leading policies on the market. Remember, every word has a meaning.

2. Loss From Sickness. The loss from sickness clause should provide protection from sickness *which first manifests itself* during the term of the policy, not sickness which is *contracted or occurs* during the term of the policy. Otherwise you may find yourself disabled from some latent disease such as tuberculosis, cancer, or heart disease that began before you took out the policy, yet be unable to collect benefits.

3. Loss From Accident. The disability shouldn't have to occur within a specific number of days from the date of the accident in order to qualify as an accident claim. Since sickness benefits are generally treated less liberally than accident benefits, it is usually to the insurance company's advantage to classify claims as sickness claims.

4. Incontestability Clause. The incontestability clause in a disability contract prevents the company from denying payment of a claim based on prior existence of a physical condition. The incontestable clause of the Series 1000 policy of Massachusetts Casualty is an example of a better clause from the insured's standpoint:

> "After this Policy has been in force for a period of two years during the lifetime of the Insured, it shall become incontestable as to the statements contained in the copy of the application. No claim for loss incurred or disability (as defined in the Policy) commencing after two years from the date of issue of this Policy shall be reduced or denied on the ground

> that a disease or physical condition not excluded
> from coverage by name or specific description effec-
> tive on the date of loss had existed prior to the
> effective date of coverage of this policy."

A weaker policy would except fraudulent misstatements
on the application from incontestability. Thus under the
weaker contract an applicant who knew he had a condition but failed to mention it on the application might be
denied payment even though the two year incontestability
period had passed.

5. **Waiver of Premium.** Better contracts will waive the
premium during periods of disability. These clauses vary from
contract to contract. Here is Paul Revere's series 811 waiver
of premium clause:

> "After total disability has continued for a period of
> 90 consecutive days, the Company will waive the
> payment of any premium which thereafter becomes
> due while the insured remains continuously totally
> disabled, and the Company will refund any premium
> paid under a disability policy which became due after
> such disability commenced."

This differs slightly from Massachusetts Casualty in that they
will refund the amount of any waived premiums which were
paid prior to the period of disability. Thus, if you had paid
an annual premium, then became disabled and the ninety day
waiting period expired, the first contract would not have
refunded the premium applying to the ninety days of
disability, while on the other hand they would pay an entire
annual premium for you had that premium fallen due while
the disability was in effect. Certain policies have no waiver of
premium at all, others have various waiting periods, some
don't refund premium, etc.

One clause to watch out for is one in which the company
only waives the premium during periods of *compensable*
disability. This would mean that if your benefit period was
two years, yet you remained disabled past the benefit period,

the waiver of premium would cease and even though you were still disabled you would have to start paying premiums again if you wanted to maintain the policy in force. Since it would be questionable as to whether you would be insurable again in such a situation, you'd probably want to keep the policy in force.

6. Presumptive Disability. Presumptive disability means that although the insured returns to work, he is still presumed to be disabled by the insurance company and would continue to receive benefits for the entire benefit period. In most contracts loss of sight, hearing, speech, or the use of two members (one hand and one foot, or two hands, etc.) qualifies the insured to receive benefits under the presumptive clause. Inferior contracts recognize only severance of the two members as presumptive disability.

7. Air Travel. Many older policies place restrictions on private flying or charter flying. All of the better policies would pay benefits for disabilities caused by any type of flying.

8. Self-Inflicted Injuries and Narcotics. Many policies exclude coverage for disabilities incurred through intentionally self-inflicted injuries or the use of narcotics except for those narcotics prescribed by a physician other than the insured. These are seemingly innocuous clauses as most policyholders don't figure they're going to intentionally injure themselves, nor do most regularly use narcotics. What about an accident that *might be construed* to be intentional? You accidentally shoot yourself in the foot while hunting. If the insurance company decides to call it an intentionally self-inflicted injury, you might have to defend yourself in court. And narcotics? Suppose you're a physician with a cold and you prescribe a mild narcotic like codine for yourself. You have an auto accident that disables you and the fact comes out that you had taken the codine. Since the clause said "... prescribed by a physician other than oneself ..." you're out of luck. Better policies do not exclude intentionally self-inflicted injuries and narcotic related disabilities from coverage. In fact in the better policies the only exclusions are war or acts of war.

9. Transplant Surgery. With the advent of popular transplant operations some companies have added a transplant donor benefit to their policies. Normally the decision to transplant an organ from your body to the body of another is a purely voluntary act. It cannot be considered a sickness nor an accident, therefore would not be covered under a normal disability policy should it cause disability. The policies, such as Massachusetts Casualty, that do cover this type of disability normally cover a transplant donor if a disability begins 12 months after the policy is in force, and restrict the benefit period to 12 months.

10. Return of Premium. Many of the disability companies have boarded the cash value bandwagon by offering a' disability policy for which the premiums will be refunded if a person doesn't become disabled for the first ten years of the policy. Naturally the premium is significantly higher for this type of coverage. This represents a bonanza for the insurance company and a loss for the policy holder. Companies that offer this feature offer it as a rider. In selling this feature the salesman will normally compare the rate of the company's regular policy and then add on the cost of the rider. Since the regular policy is a higher priced policy, it makes the cost of the return of premium feature seem relatively small. As a matter of fact, the salesman will be able to show you that the extra premium you'll be paying will compound itself at 12% or 13% per year for the ten year period, and if you don't get disabled you'll collect a healthy profit. He fails to mention that by going to another company you could purchase the base policy without the rider for significantly less than his company is offering it, thus lowering the hypothetical rate of return. Additionally, if you get disabled during the ten year period the company will deduct the amount of any benefit payments made to you from the refund.

No one likes to see insurance money go down the drain,

and the idea of getting it back if you stay healthy is attractive. Under one company's rider if an insured has no claims during a ten year period the company will refund 80% of the total premiums paid during the period. If you have a disability claim that totals less than 20% of the ten year's premiums the company deducts the amount paid in claims from the refund at the end of the period. If your claims during the period total more than 20% of the ten year's premiums, you get no refund, but a new ten year period commences. In case number one, let's assume that the premium is $1,000 per year for $2,000 per month of coverage with a 30 day waiting period, and you have a disability that lasts 90 days. If you put in a claim, you will receive $4,000 in benefits, but you will receive no refund of premium for the period. The premium you paid for that benefit was twice as high as you should have paid. Naturally, even if you have a disability you won't file a claim because by collecting that $4,000 you would forfeit the $8,000 refund of premium. In fact, if you were anywhere near the end of your ten year period you'd be foolish to put in any claim unless it was for at least the $8,000 potential refund.

The insurance company has effectively caused you to insure yourself. Another way to look at it is that they've sold you a policy with a 30-day wait, but because of the penalty to you, you really have a policy with a five-month waiting period.

Even if you don't get disabled and get a refund of 80% of your premium, what is the net result? The company has held the money for the ten year period. In the meantime if inflation continues at 12% per year, the 80% refund will have a value of $4,500.

In short, return of premium is something to shy away from. It's bad news.

Step-Rate Policies

In order to compete in the young professional market, one of the most lucrative markets in the disability field, companies have come out with step-rate policies which offer low premiums for the first five years, with the premiums then stepping up to regular rates. A young professional age 35 or under now has the option of buying a regular policy at a constant premium for the life of the policy, or the step rate. As an example Springfield Life offers its Select Step Rate Policy. A male professional, age 30, could buy a $1,000 per month benefit with a 30-day wait and age-65 benefit period for an initial premium of $231 per year, stepping up to $424 after five years. Or he. could buy their regular policy for a straight $367 per year. Inasmuch as disability premiums are falling every year due to competition and higher medical technology, it would be advisable to take the lower premium if available. By the time the rate steps up, you may be able to transfer to an even cheaper policy.

Salesmen, working on commission as they do, frequently forget to mention the step-rate plans as the commission is substantially lower. If you're under 35, be sure you inquire.

Comparing Price

Premiums for essentially equally structured contracts vary immensely from company to company, so once you've decided on what you want, don't buy from the first company that comes along. The companies that specialize in the disability income field generally offer the best contracts at the lowest prices, but even among the specialists there is a great price difference depending on the benefits you want and your age. It's been my experience that the bigger life insurance companies tend to have the highest premiums in the disability income insurance field. Four companies that currently offer excellent contracts at low rates are Paul Revere, Springfield, Massachusetts Casualty (not to be confused with Massachusetts Mutual or Massachusetts Indemnity) and Provident Life & Accident Insurance Company.

Summary

Disability income insurance is one of the most important types of insurance you can carry. Its purchase should be approached in the same way you approach the purchase of life insurance. Determine the amount you need, how long a benefit you need, and how long you can wait before the benefit starts. Then compare the contracts and prices of a variety of companies. Don't *underinsure*, and, as in life insurance, review your coverage at least every two years.

CHAPTER FIVE

The Income Tax

Hardly any area in money management is as filled with mysticism and misunderstanding as is tax planning. It's mind-boggling to listen to taxpayers who have paid in hundreds of thousands of dollars in income taxes who still don't understand what a tax bracket is, and whose only tax planning input comes from people who are unqualified to be speaking on the subject. Hardly any area of wealth accumulation is as potentially rewarding as the tax area. The decision on whether to try and reduce taxes is yours to make. If you feel justified in doing so, I'll try to organize the subject so that you can understand it and accomplish the job with minimum energy and maximum efficiency.

Income is taxed on a graduated scale, the higher the income, the higher the percentage paid in tax; but this does *not* mean that a person in a 50% tax bracket pays 50% of his or her income in tax. For a married taxpayer on the first $1,000 of taxable income you pay $140 tax (14%) on the second thousand you pay $150 (15%) on the third thousand you pay $160 (16%) and so on up. The rate begins to jump in irregular intervals and when you reach $44,000 of taxable income it stops increasing. A married taxpayer with a taxable income of $44,000 will pay 50% of the dollars *above* $44,000 in tax and thus he is said to be in a 50% federal tax bracket. But he does not pay 50% of the $44,000 to the IRS,

but rather $14,060 or about 32%. The maximum federal
bracket is 50% only on "earned" income from your
occupation. If you have unearned income from investments
the bracket goes on up to 70%.

So much for federal tax brackets. In addition most states
levy an income tax which varies from state to state and is
usually graduated like the federal but at lower percentages. In
California the maximum is 11% on incomes in excess of
$31,000 for married persons.

Those who have relatively small incomes think that anyone
with a high income can simply go to his accountant, pull a
few strings and voila, there's a fancy tax shelter that
eliminates taxes. Anyone in a high tax bracket knows this is
far from the truth. There is no legal avoidance, merely
postponement and conversion to lower brackets.

There are two main categories of income that can be
protected from taxation; income from your present occupation, and income from your investments. In this book I'm
not going to cover tax shelters for investment income, but
only the single most important shelter: a qualified retirement
plan.

QUALIFIED RETIREMENT PLANS

There are two possibilities; you are an employee of a
company or you're self-employed. If you're a corporate
employee your income comes in the form of a salary or wage,
and the whole thing must be reported as taxable income. You
might be able to induce your employer (especially if you own
the business) to make expenditures that will ultimately
accrue to your benefit, rather than currently paying these
monies out to you as salary. Assuming these purchases are
tax deductible to the corporation and not currently taxable
to you, you have effectively lowered your taxable income by
the amount of the corporation expenditure. There are several
things that fall into this category but the most important are
corporate pension and profit-sharing plans.

In these plans the company makes a contribution to a
trustee who takes the money and holds it or invests it at the
direction of you or a committee appointed by your employer. The contribution is a deductible business expense to
the employer, but since it is placed in the hands of a trustee
and not released to you until normal retirement age, it is not
deemed to be part of your salary until you actually receive it.
If you're in a 50% tax bracket and receive $1,000 in salary
you'll pay $500 in taxes and have only $500 left to invest. If
the employer contributes the same $1,000 to a plan, the
entire $1,000 can be invested and you'll have the earnings on
the whole amount accruing to you over a period of time. The
difference between the amount you'd have left if you
received the income direct, paid the tax, and invested the
difference, and the amount you would accumulate if you
invested the pretax amount and compounded it at the full
pretax compounding rate, will be a profit to you for having
participated in the plan.

Under current law the amount the corporation can
contribute depends on the type of plans set up. There are
two qualified plans, the pension plan (which can be either a
defined benefit plan or a defined contribution plan) and the
profit-sharing plan.

DEFINED-BENEFIT PENSION PLANS

A defined-benefit pension plan is a plan designed to give an
employee a fixed monthly income at some preselected
retirement age. For example, the corporation decides that
normal retirement age is 65, and that it will provide any
employee who stays with the corporation a sufficient length
of time with a retirement salary equal to 75% of his salary at
the time of retirement. Thus if the employee is making
$2,000 a month when he reaches age 65, the retirement fund
will pay out to him $1,500 a month for the rest of his life.

In order to calculate the amount of money that must be

contributed to this plan, actuarial calculations are required. The actuary takes into consideration the number of years before the employee's retirement, the salary being earned by the employee, the number of years the employee is likely to live after retirement, and the estimated rate of return the trust will be able to earn on the money deposited. From these inputs he calculates how much money should be deposited each year for that employee.

In some cases corporations will not hire actuaries directly, but will simply purchase retirement-income insurance policies or annuities from insurance companies, in which case the insurance company is taking on the job of making these calculations.

Under current law there is no precise limit to the amount of money that can be put away for a corporate employee to fund a defined benefit pension plan. Each plan is submitted to the IRS for approval and they have the right to disqualify it if they feel that it discriminates among the employees unfairly, or if it allows for too great a retirement benefit.

Defined benefit plans can be particularly beneficial to high income professionals. A 55-year-old doctor with a net practice income of $100,000 per year could incorporate and set up such a plan that will pay him 100% of salary at age 65. He could set his salary at $50,000 per year and contribute the other $50,000 to the retirement plan. Thus over 10 years he would accumulate $500,000 in the plan plus interest, and under the right set of actuarial assumptions this could fund his total salary on retirement. His income taxes drop substantially, of course, as now instead of being taxed on the entire $100,000 of practice income, he is only taxed on $50,000 of salary.

The first drawback to a defined-benefit plan would be the fact that a contribution must be made to the plan every year, even if the corporation does not show a profit. The only exception would be in the case a plan were terminated.

Defined-beneift plans have the further drawback that the amount of future contributions cannot be accurately estimated when the plan is initiated. Poor investment performance of the funds might require much larger contributions in the later years of the plan in order to meet the promised pensions.

DEFINED-CONTRIBUTION PENSION PLANS

If a corporation doesn't want to hire actuaries to calculate its plan contributions, or the uncertainty of varying future contributions, but still wants the advantages of tax deductible contributions to a retirement plan, it can set up a defined-contribution pension plan. Here the annual contribution to the plan is a fixed percentage of each covered employee's salary, up to a maximum of $25,000. The percentage of salary is limited to 25% and the same percentage of salary must apply to all employees; thus the doctor who would put away 25% of his salary must also contribute 25% of his nurse's salary to the plan for her benefit. The ultimate retirement income available to an employee will not be a fixed percentage of salary, as in the defined-benefit plan, but rather will depend on the size to which the fund has grown at retirement. Thus, if the contributions are invested wisely, the employee's retirement check would be bigger, and if they are invested foolishly, he might wind up with very little. One should realize that under the defined-benefit plan the money could be invested unwisely also, but if the fund consistently lost money, the corporation would be obligated to make larger contributions to make up for the fund's poor performance.

PROFIT-SHARING PLANS

A profit-sharing plan is supposedly set up to let the employees of a corporation participate in the profits of the company. Ostensibly its functions are twofold: to give the employees an incentive to produce more efficiently by sharing in the profits generated, and to provide them an additional retirement benefit. For most small corporations, the plan is not used as an incentive to employees but rather as another method of reducing the taxes of the stockholder-employees. The corporation is allowed to contribute an amount equal to up to 15% of the compensation of eligible employees, and deduct the contribution as a business expense. The money is put into a trust fund and invested until the employee's retirement, at which time it is distributed to him, either in a lump sum or in installments. The employee doesn't declare it as income until it's actually received. Unlike the pension plan, the corporation is not obligated to make an annual contribution to a profit-sharing plan. The board of directors determines the profits at the end of each fiscal year and makes a decision on the size of contribution. This feature makes the profit-sharing plan somewhat more attractive to small corporations in which the amount of available capital is uncertain from one year to the next.

A company setting up a profit-sharing plan can also contribute to a pension plan, but when two plans are in existence at one time, they are limited to a total contribution of 25% of each employee's compensation, or $25,000, whichever is less. Thus with both plans in effect and 15% being contributed to the profit sharing plan, only 10% could be contributed to the pension plan. Most professional corporations or other closely held corporations tend to prefer a combination of the two plans in that they have the option to put as much as 25% of salary away each year, but are only obligated to put away the 10% that represents the pension plan.

Vesting

The vesting period of a plan is the period during which an employee must work for a company before being entitled to withdraw his retirement plan monies upon termination. The

IRS tends to favor shorter vesting periods, especially in smaller corporations in which the stockholder employees have a large share of the profit-sharing fund. Typically a professional corporation will set a vesting schedule which will vest pension plans at the rate of 10% per year and profit-sharing plans at the rate of 20% per year, thus they would be totally vested over five or ten years. The owner of a small corporation might prefer to let the participants' accounts vest even more rapidly. The faster the better as far as the IRS is concerned.

Trustees

Both pension and profit-sharing plans require that the funds contributed be held by a trustee in trust for the participants. The function of the trustee is to take the funds from the corporation, record their receipt, invest them in whatever the investment committee tells it to invest them in, hold the securities purchased, and record all transactions that occur. Currently the trustee must file form 990-P and provide the information to the corporation to enable the corporation to file forms 4848, 4848-A and 4849 with its federal income tax return.

While the corporation may set up an investment committee whose function is to determine where the plan funds are to be invested, their directions to the trustee may be ignored if the trustee in his judgment believes that the recommended investment would either violate the rules of prudent investment judgment, or would disqualify the plan's deductibility in the eyes of the IRS. Typically, banks and trust companies are set up to act in the capacity of trustee for retirement plans, and the majority of the plans in the country are trusteed by such institutions. However, there is nothing that precludes any individual from acting as the trustee of a plan, and many professionals do act as their own trustee. The only problem with doing this is that an individual, untutored in the role of trustee, might inadvertently disqualify a plan by failing to adhere to the rules and regulations. On the other hand, the services of a professional trustee are expensive, and in smaller plans the costs significantly eat into the tax savings of the program.

You must look carefully at the source of the recommendations you get in this area, as in any other. Many lawyers rely heavily on the referrals they get from banks and trust companies, and to promote the idea that a person can act as his own trustee is likely to result in offending his sources. Like most other things however, you can do it yourself and cheaply.

Administration

In addition to the function performed by the trustee, there are certain other services required that fall under the heading of administration. They consist of determining the amount that should be contributed to the plan each fiscal year, how that is to be allocated among the employees, informing each employee as to his vested interest in the plan, and filling out forms 4848 and 4849 for the corporation federal tax return. These tasks can be handled by the corporate bookkeeper or farmed out to companies that specialize in the administration of this type of trust.

Funding

Pension and profit-sharing funds can be invested in a variety of ways. They can be used to purchase:

Savings Accounts
Time Certificates
Bonds, Corporate and Government
Preferred Stocks
Common Stocks
Mutual Funds
Life Insurance

    Limited Partnership Interests
    Real Estate

That isn't to say that the trustee of your plan will automatically purchase these things on the request of the investment committee. To the contrary, most trustees will look at several factors before investing.

1. Is it prudent? The Prudent Man rule says that the trustee can be liable for losses if he invests the money in something that a "Prudent Man" would not have invested in, all things considered. This is a vague rule that would probably come into play if the participant in a plan decided to sue for breach of fiduciary responsibility in the event of loss of trust funds. Nevertheless, in most states trustees are bound by this rule, and in the case of any unusual investments will always try to determine the merits of the investment.

2. Is it liquid? Inasmuch as participants in retirement plans occasionally retire, quit, become disabled or die, there are periodic needs to dispurse portions of the funds. A trustee will want a substantial part of the monies in the plan to be in readily marketable investments such as common stocks, bonds, and savings accounts in order to meet these payments.

3. Is the investment a problem in terms of paperwork or handling? Trustees like to deal with simple paperwork transactions. Most will not get involved with storing things like gold coins, or investigating the merits of small offerings. The fees they charge just aren't enough to justify anything but investments that can be handled routinely.

4. Is the investment a business to be operated directly or indirectly by the plan? If a pension plan owns a business then the income from that business will not be tax free, as is the income from other passive investments. It will be treated as unrelated business income and taxed to the plan. While this type of investment will not disqualify the plan, it does make the plan lose some of its attraction as a shelter.

Life Insurance

Of the things available to a pension plan as an investment, what are most logical? Well, certain things can be eliminated right off. One of the most common vehicles for plan funding is life insurance. The insurance companies of the United States have developed immense divisions to do nothing but sell life insurance to pension plans. Their arguments to justify these sales follow these lines:

1. The growth is guaranteed. It's risk free.
2. The insurance portion of the whole life is taxable to the employee, but at favorable rates.
3. The death benefit is free of estate tax.
4. You're buying your insurance with pre-tax dollars.
5. The insurance company provides the actuarial services free or at a very low cost.

That list is by no means complete, as you well know if you've ever been approached by an insurance agent regarding pension plans. Let's examine it point by point.

1. The growth is guaranteed. Right, you get a guaranteed 3 to 4% return on the invested funds. Let's face it, in a conventional cash value insurance policy outside a plan the 3% return has some tax advantage in that the income isn't taxed. But inside the plan income wouldn't be taxed anyway. Why not a bank savings account, or better still, treasury bills, guaranteed, by the U.S. Government that might double the yield of the life insurance contract but still give you the safety you want? They shouldn't say the growth is guaranteed, they should say *the loss* is guaranteed because that's exactly what you'll have in our present economy if you put your funds to work at 3 or 4%.

Of course the insurance agent will counter that the true rate of return on the insurance policy is effectively double because the contribution to the plan was tax deductible. Of course, but the true return of *any* investment made with those dollars would be doubled by the same token. When considering returns, look at your pension or profit-sharing dollars as an isolated fund, not affected by the fact that it was contributed to the plan originally. In reality, it is simply part of your overall net worth; part of your investable assets. Would you buy cash value insurance if it were outside the plan?

2. The fact that the term insurance portion of the premium is taxable income to the employee at favorable rates is no advantage to buying insurance within the plan; it simply raises the cost and defines the problem by illustrating that you are really just making an investment in the cash value portion of the contract with those pension funds. By buying that term insurance portion of the contract with plan dollars you are lowering the available dollars in the plan with which you can build an investment portfolio. If those premium dollars were put to work in investments, you would have that many more investment dollars growing tax-deferred.

3. The death benefit is free of estate tax, true, but there are other ways this can be accomplished even buying your insurance outside the plan. For example, you can make someone other than the insured the owner of the policy, thus taking the proceeds out of the estate of the decedent. Even if you considered this to be a benefit, it can be measured in dollars (the dollars required to buy the additional amount of insurance to fund the taxes), and you would probably find the dollar benefit didn't significantly raise the true rate of return on the investment in the policy.

Another point to remember: while life insurance proceeds are not taxable to the estate, neither are any other assets held in the plan.

4. You're buying your insurance with pre-tax dollars, all right, but by doing so you are *not* able to buy other investments with those pre-tax dollars. This argument simply overlooks the fact that you either buy insurance in the plan and investments outside the plan or vice-versa. You'd be far better off buying investments within the plan, since one of the major advantages of a pension plan to begin with is the fact that investment income is not taxed. Always compare the investment with what else could be done with those same dollars in the plan.

5. Granted they do provide actuarial services at a low cost, because the actual cost is built into the profits they make by being able to borrow your cash value at 3% interest and lend it out at 12%. Since most smaller corporations would be better off with a defined-contribution plan in which no actuaries are involved, this savings may not exist.

What about other disadvantages of buying insurance in a plan? How about the losses of capital involved when employees terminate in the early years of their employment? Remember, cash value builds slowly in the first couple of years of a policy, and if the employee quits that premium that was paid and not credited to cash value is lost to the remaining participants. Had those premiums been invested in bonds, stocks or savings accounts, nothing would have been lost.

Plans set up with a provision for a certain percentage of the plan contribution to go into insurance initiate a cycle that is increasingly wasteful. Every time the salaries of employees go up, new policies on those employees are purchased by the plan. Over a period of time, an employee finds his insurance coverage going up and up. This would be fine if the person were underinsured, but most people aren't.

In fact, most people don't bother to cancel out their personal policies when they become insured under a pension plan and wind up paying for twice as much insurance as they really need.

Conclusion

Don't buy insurance through a pension or profit-sharing plan except under the following circumstances:

1. You can't afford to make the maximum contribution to the plan except by cancelling your personal insurance policies and rebuying the insurance within the plan. In this case it might make sense in order to get that deduction.

2. You're uninsurable and have a chance to pick up some additional insurance without a physical.

3. You like to throw money away.

Other Investments

One of the advantages of placing money into a qualified retirement plan is that dividends, interest, and capital gains are not taxed until the money is distributed at death, disability or retirement. Therefore, it makes sense to utilize this feature by making your pension fund the vehicle for those types of investments that normally yield taxable income. In any well planned portfolio there are a variety of types of investments used. A person should have assets in all the major categories like store of value, loans, investments, etc. Balancing a portfolio means diversifying your assets in such a way as to hedge against all the major economic and financial risks that were outlined in Chapter II.

Since certain of these assets yield taxable income and certain do not, it makes sense to buy income-yielding investments through your pension or profit-sharing plan while buying those that don't carry a taxable yield outside the plan. Coins and bullion for example, earn no interest whatsoever. They are passive store-of-value assets. Carrying them in the plan while at the same time keeping a substantial savings account or high-dividend-yielding stock outside the plan is not sensible. Likewise real estate limited partnerships frequently throw off tax-free returns, as do municipal bonds. All of these would be more beneficially carried outside the plan where their tax advantages could be most fully utilized, while types of securities with high yield could be used within the plan.

Secrecy is another consideration. Many investors would like to have as little of their business as possible open to scrutiny; some because they fear the possibility of state confiscation of property as economic conditions worsen; some because they want to minimize taxes to whatever extent possible; some because they just don't want their spouse or business associates to know what they're doing. A person can buy gold coins for cash, store them in a secret place here or abroad, and sell them for cash when needed. The transaction is not recorded, and if gains are made no one is the wiser. This can be done outside a pension plan, but not within the trust.

The Most Suitable

The best investments to put into the pension or profit-sharing trust are those which would take the maximum advantage of the tax-free nature of the vehicle. Assets in which you expect to realize large capital gains for example. This allows you to postpone the taxes on the gain. The trust would be a good vehicle in which to play stock market strategies that required substantial short term trading. Remember, you shouldn't go into any investment within the pension trust that you wouldn't plan to use assuming you had no trust.

The first step in developing a rational wealth-accumulation strategy is to design a balanced investment portfolio that will accomplish your financial goals while protecting you against risks. After the design is complete, then decide which of the selected assets would most logically be owned by the trust.

The Payout

Under current IRS regulations a participant in a pension or profit-sharing plan gets favorable tax treatment on distribution of the trust. In situations where the employee has made no contributions to the plan, and all funds were employer contributions made after 1973, if the recipient takes the distribution as a lump sum payment in one tax year, the total distribution is taxable and the tax is figured by taking ten times the tax (using the single person's tax rate table) on 1/10 of the total taxable amount. This represents a sort of ten year averaging, and is based on the theory that a person lives for about ten years after normal (age 65) retirement.

Another alternative is to take the payments from the trust over a number of years. This usually results in an even more favorable situation for the participant. The trust is maintained in force, and the capital accumulated within it continues to earn. The payments made to an individual are all taxable income to him, but look at how this might work in a hypothetical situation in which invested funds are earning 10%.

	Lump Sum Payout	Income Payout
Accumulation In Plan	$250,000	$250,000
Lump Sum Distribution	$250,000	$ 0
Tax On Distribution	72,000	0
Capital Balance	$178,000	$250,000
Annual Income from Capital	$ 17,800	$ 25,000
Tax on Income	4,000	6,000
Net Spendable	$ 13,800	$ 19,000

The IRS would require that a percentage of the principal of the account be paid to the participant each year in order to amortize the plan capital out over the participant's life expectancy. Even so, the benefit is substantially greater to the participant if the total amount of the accumulated capital can be left working.

The above statements regarding payouts from a qualified plan aren't meant to cover the subject in any depth; there are many complicating factors. Payout rules should be carefully reviewed when the plan is set up.

Covering Other Employees

When a small corporation considers setting up a qualified retirement plan one of the primary considerations is the ultimate tax savings to the stockholder-employees. If any other employees must be covered under the plan, this subtracts from the tax benefits enjoyed. This loss can be partially offset by proper structuring of waiting periods and vesting schedules.

The waiting period is that period of time after a person is hired before he becomes eligible to have a contribution made on his behalf by the corporation. The law limits this period to a maximum of one year except in cases where there is 100% vesting after three years, in which case a three year waiting period is acceptable. Waiting periods must apply equally to all employees including stockholders.

Vesting Periods

It would be to the advantage of the stockholder employees to have as long a vesting period as possible in order to recycle as much of the employer's contributions as possible back to the fund and eventually to the stockholder employees (who in most cases would tend to outlast the regular employees).

In a pension plan, amounts forfeited by terminating employees are allocated to the remaining plan participants on a pro-rata basis, but additionally reduce the corporate contribution by the amount of the forfeiture in the year it occurs. Thus there is no real advantage to the plan participants, but the corporation is that much richer by not having to make the contribution. In profit-sharing plans, the forfeitures accrue directly to the accounts of the other plan participants on a pro-rata basis, and this forfeiture does not affect the corporate contribution for the year. So the plan participants get the windfall of the forfeiture, and a regular yearly contribution as well.

Social Security Integration

One way in which stockholder employees can increase their share of the annual corporate plan contribution at the expense of the other employees is by integrating the plan with social security. The law recognizes the fact that the entire salary of lower paid employees is covered by social security benefits, while higher paid employees are only covered for the first $13,200 of income; thus lower paid employees might have most or all their income covered with social security while the higher paid employees would not. In order to equalize this discrepancy, it allows a pension or profit-sharing plan to allocate a portion of the corporate contribution to the portion of salaries in excess of $13,200 before the contribution is divided up among the plan participants. This is a feature that shouldn't be overlooked in the drafting of a pension or profit-sharing plan.

How To Set One Up

If you're incorporated and haven't yet installed a pension or profit-sharing plan, you should carefully investigate the idea of doing so. The first step is to find a competent corporation/tax attorney who has had significant experience in setting up professional corporations. Since these corporations are usually set up with the tax benefits of pension plans as their primary motive, an attorney that specializes in this area will be most familiar with tax laws and benefits from

your point of view. He'll be able to guide you to the proper
trustee, and administrator.

It would probably be wise to seek advice on what
investments to buy with plan assets from outside sources as
this is generally not the forte of tax attorneys. Be extremely
wary if your attorney introduces you to any insurance
salesmen. Inasmuch as insurance men direct a lot of business
to attorneys, there is often a need to reciprocate, and
attorneys will frequently push insurance funded plans for just
that reason.

If your business is not incorporated, you might find it
profitable to explore incorporation simply for the tax
benefits offered by qualified pension and profit-sharing plans.
In order to help you make your own calculations about the
net economic effect of incorporation, pages 249 and 250 in
the Appendix will be useful.

A PENSION PLAN FOR THE SELF-EMPLOYED

In 1962 congress passed the "Keogh" bill, sometimes
known as the H.R. 10 bill, which made it possible for
individuals who are self-employed to set up retirement
plans for themselves and enjoy some of the tax benefits
formerly only available to corporate employees. While not as
liberal as the corporate plans, these Keogh plans are
extremely lucrative from a tax standpoint.

Who Can Contribute to a Keogh Plan?

Anyone who has income from self-employment can
contribute. Thus a commission salesman, a physician, dentist,
small businessman, farmer, or just about anyone who is not
an employee of another person or corporation can set up a
plan. In cases where a person has income from two sources, it
might be possible to have a Keogh plan covering one source
and not the other. For example a school teacher might be in
business as a consultant as well as being employed by some
school district. If the income received from consulting does
not pass through the school district, then a portion of that

income could be contributed to the plan. If a professional incorporates in the middle of the year, any income received by him prior to incorporation is considered income from self-employment, and a contribution to a Keogh plan could be made for that year even though he might subsequently set up a corporate retirement plan.

How Much Can Be Contributed?

Under the legislation recently passed by Congress and signed by President Ford, a self-employed individual can contribute 15% of his net business income up to a maximum of $7,500. This contribution is considered to have been made on the last day of the plan year, providing it is made not later than the day authorized for filing the return (including extensions). The entire contribution, up to the maximum limit above, is deductible and thus could save the taxpayer up to $3,750 on his federal taxes.

In addition to the above mentioned tax-deductible contribution, a participant in a Keogh plan can make a "voluntary" contribution to the plan of up to 10% of his net self-employment income up to a maximum of $2,500. This voluntary contribution is not deductible, but once the money is in the plan, the income or capital gains earned by that money is not taxable to the participant until it is taken out of the plan. Thus a person who is currently keeping some of his assets in non-sheltered, income producing situations could transfer them into the plan via the voluntary contribution and save the taxes on the income those assets were producing.

The above voluntary contribution is not possible for a self-employed person unless that person has one or more employees who are also covered under the plan.

Employees

If a self-employed person has employees, it may be necessary to make contributions for those employees. According to the regulations he must initially include in the plan all full time employees with 3 or more years of service. His employees are considered full time if their customary employment is more than 1000 hours a year. If the owner-employee has less than three years service himself, then the waiting period is reduced accordingly.

The contribution for the covered employees must be a percentage of their salary equal to the percentage contributed for the owner-employee. Thus if the owner has an income of $75,000 per year and contributes $7,500 for himself, since that contribution is 10% of his compensation, he must contribute 10% of the compensation of each eligible employee. The contribution made for the employee vests immediately and that employee will have the right to withdraw it upon termination.

What Becomes of the Money?

The law allows you to put away money for your retirement providing that's what you do with the money. To insure that you don't misappropriate the funds from your own retirement plan, you are required to give those funds to a trustee. Once the money is in the hands of the trustee you can tell that trustee what to do with it. You can direct that it be held in cash, placed in a savings account, used to buy bonds, stocks, treasury bills, mortgages, or life insurance. In other words, the money can be invested in much the same way you might invest it if it were not in the plan. The only difference is that you must work through the trustee.

Your selection of a trustee or custodian bank depends to a certain extent on what you intend to do with the funds once they're in the plan. Since trustees are in business for a profit you'll have to pay a fee to get them to handle your plan, and they'll get remunerated based on the amount of work involved and the risk to themselves. Certain organizations will act as trustee for your funds for little or no fee, just in order to have access to your funds. Life insurance companies, mutual funds, and some Savings & Loans and banks will offer to let you use their prototype plan document, and to act as trustee or custodian providing you buy their product with the money. If you want flexibility with your funds, that is, if you want to invest in several different products or want the ability to move from one investment to another, then you'll have to hire a trustee that will allow you to do this. Here the fee will be higher, naturally. Below are listed three independent trustees that charge a fee and allow some diversification of investments:

Lincoln Trust Company
P.O. Box 5831
Denver, Colorado 80217

First Trust Corporation
444 Sherman
Denver, Colorado

Certified Plans, Inc.
P.O. Box 2090
Newport Beach, California 92663

If you'd prefer to act as your own trustee, the 1974 Pension Reform Act made this possible. You'll need to have a good tax attorney draft the plan for you and advise you as to your responsibilities as trustee.

What Should Keogh Plans Invest In?

The same philosophy that guided corporate pension plan strategy applies to Keogh as well. Since all income is tax deferred within the plan, this would not be the place for tax-sheltered types of investments like municipal bonds or real estate. Since life insurance is low yielding and tax deferred, there is no sense to putting it in a Keogh plan. If you plan to keep certain of your assets in fixed income loans, this would be a good place to put them, as the income wouldn't be diminished by taxation. It would be a good place, also, to do any securities trading, as short- and long-term gains would also be sheltered.

When Can I Get My Money Out?

Anytime you want it. If you take a distribution from the plan prior to age 59½, then you'll have to pay 10% of the money in the plan as a tax penalty, plus having to add the entire amount to your taxable income in the year of the distribution. For that reason you'd probably be wise to leave the money in the plan until retirement. The penalty does not apply to your voluntary contributions, however. Since you've already paid taxes on them you can withdraw them without penalty, so long as you leave their earnings in the plan.

How Do I Set Up a Plan?

Simply write to any of the above mentioned trustees and they'll send you complete information along with enrollment forms. If you prefer to act as your own trustee, contact an attorney.

Summary

The most logical tax-shelters available today are qualified retirement plans. If you're an employee of a corporation you may be covered by either a pension plan, a profit-sharing plan, or both. If you're an employee of your own corporation, check into setting up these plans if you haven't already done so. If you're self-employed, you're eligible to set up a Keogh plan, and if you don't have one, you should. For those who are employed and their employers have neither a corporate plan nor a Keogh, the 1974 Pension Reform Law establishes an individual retirement account in which a person who is not covered by any other retirement plan can contribute 15% of income up to a maximum of $1,500 per year into a retirement account. This account is similar to the Keogh plan, except one cannot act as his own trustee.

If you don't have a qualified retirement plan yet, set one up this year. You need those tax savings more than the government needs the taxes.

CHAPTER SIX

Putting It All Together

It's time to look back over your shoulder and survey the road you've followed. By now you should have a good idea of the elements that make our economy work. Production is the basis of all that improves our standard of living, and anything that tends to interfere with production reduces our standard of living. You should be painfully aware of the reasons behind our current inflation and its personal effects on you.

You should have outlined and calculated your financial objectives, and know roughly how many years you have to accomplish them. You've read about the variety of risks facing you in your search for financial independence, and should have some idea of which ones you feel are most threatening.

You have been exposed to the three basic types of investments; store of value, loans, and equities. You know that you can invest in these assets, or you can speculate in them by buying for short term profits.

Now the question you must be asking yourself is, "How do I determine which of these assets is most suited to my portfolio?" How do you structure the optimum investment portfolio to meet your goals? The balance of this chapter will give you some step by step instructions.

Step One—Invest in Yourself

Before you place money with others for growth, make certain you have fully funded your own business. That is your soundest investment. You have control, vested interest and maximum profit.

Step Two—Set Up Qualified Retirement Plans

Before you decide on which investment assets you should own, establish any qualified retirement programs and other tax-deferred trusts that can conserve tax dollars for your own use. Then when you balance your portfolio you can decide which assets should be placed in the trusts and which carried outside. These programs, as outlined in Chapter 5, will be Keogh plans and pension or profit sharing plans.

Step Three—Tally Your Investable Assets and Surplus

From your financial statement you should be able to calculate the total investable assets that you have available. Identify the type of investment in each case, i.e., store of value, loan, or equity, and determine whether each asset is held as an investment or speculation. From your monthly Income & Expense sheet you should be able to determine how much investable surplus will be added to your net worth each year.

Step Four—Decide on the Ideal Portfolio Balance

Now decide what percentage of your total assets should be invested in each category of assets. This depends on your own assessment of the future of our economy, and the rate of return you need to reach your goals.

Following is an example of a percentage allocation of assets.

Store of Value 60%
Loans 5%
Equities
    Liquid 20%
    Non-Liquid 15%

Total   100%

The amount of these assets that are speculatively invested will depend on the size of your holdings in relation to your ultimate need for capital. You shouldn't speculate with money that will be essential to meeting your goals on schedule. By the same token, if you have already accumulated enough wealth to last you for the rest of your life, then there would be no sense in speculating at all.

As economic conditions change, you might alter the portfolio balance. In a stable economy that is not suffering from inflation, a conservative stance would be to invest two-thirds of your assets in equities and one third in loans. If our economy slides into true hyper-inflation, you would want no loans at all, and probably no equities, with the possible exception of your own business.

Step Five—Balance Your Portfolio

Look at the present structure of your assets and think about how you can bring it into line with the balance that you think is correct. It will mean liquidating certain assets and buying others. You can also bring the portfolio into line by adding your annual surplus to the category that is underfunded.

Figure 21 is a hypothetical case which shows how you might categorize your assets as they are now, and as you think they should be in light of our discussions in this book.

Asset	Current Allocation	Proposed Allocation
Store of Value		
Cash, Checking Accounts	$ 1,500	$ -0-
Raw Land	7,000	7,000
Gold, Silver	-0-	35,000
Furs, Jewelry	2,500	2,500
Total Store of Value	$ 11,000	$ 44,500
Loans		
Savings & Loan	$ 12,000	$ 2,000
Life Ins. Cash Value	7,600	-0-
U.S. Government Bonds	3,000	-0-
Second Trust Deed	4,700	-0-
Total Loans	$ 27,300	$ 2,000
Equities		
Dental Practice	$ 50,000	$ 50,000
Common Stocks	13,000	-0-
Apartment House Syndication	10,000	-0-
Home (Equity only)	20,000	20,000
Total Equities	$ 93,000	$ 70,000
TOTAL	$131,300	$131,300

Figure 21

Step Six—Pay Off Loans

In today's economy one of the individual's greatest risks is that sudden changes in economic conditions can create liquidity crises. Even though by borrowing money today you can benefit from inflation by paying off the loans with inflated currency, you can also be wiped out if unable to meet the payments. The most conservative position is to eliminate debt. Pay off mortgages, auto loans, and investment margin accounts. Although the rate of return on your investments may seem to drop when this is done, so will the risk of total loss of the equity.

Step Seven—Determine Investment Strategy in Advance

The most important piece of advice that can be given is that you should never invest on the spur of the moment without having first determined that the investment is consistent with your overall plan. You should determine at the beginning of each year just how much surplus you'll have available that year to invest, and in what categories the monies should be invested to properly meet your long range goals. By making careful income and expense estimates for the coming year, you should know what your total income tax liability will be, and you should be able to take full advantage of any available tax shelters by allocating a portion of your after-tax surplus to the purchase of tax-favored investments. I'm assuming of course that the first consideration is not the tax aspect, but rather the need for that type of investment to fill out your portfolio balance.

When approached by a silver-tongued salesman, first categorize the type of investment. Is what he's offering you a store-of-value, loan, or equity? Is he offering it on an investment or speculative basis? Margin or no margin? When that's determined, does your portfolio have a need for that particular type? If not, is this one good enough to replace a similar investment in the same category that you're already holding, and if so, can you liquidate your present asset and then replace it with this one?

Most people never take this systematic approach to making investment decisions. They look at each offering as a separate decision that bears no relationship to their previous decisions.

Nothing could be more wrong or potentially dangerous. Your investments are all inter-related; your program must be carefully integrated; your decisions must be coordinated.

In summary, there is no single "perfect asset". To survive you must diversify, stay as liquid as possible, and become intimately aware of the economic conditions of the world. Above all, you must have a plan. Every investment decision must relate back to that plan, and you must review and update that plan constantly.

CHAPTER SEVEN

Conclusion

Where will the economy of the United States go in the next ten or twenty years? There are many prophets around to answer that question. Some foresee a continuation of the past with minor ups and downs. These are the establishment spokesmen who say that if we can hold on, support our president, and have confidence, all the economic battles will be won: inflation will be licked, industry will prosper, unemployment will vanish, and everyone will live happily ever after. Other prophets see runaway inflation followed by catastrophic depression. After that, rioting, starvation, and anarchy. They exhort you to prepare for the holocaust: store food, guns, and plenty of silver and gold to use for barter. All would have you believe that the spectrum of possibilities lies somewhere in between these viewpoints.

I, for one, don't believe either outcome is possible. The government, in order to survive, must pursue policies contrary to those that would solve the problems. There is *no* possibility that any actions can or will be taken by this or any administration that would stop inflation or improve the standard of living of the nation. At best the actions of Governments of the world will simply redistribute the wealth; the friction they cause while doing this will lower the productive output of the people and thereby lower their standards of living.

Nevertheless, the failure of these policies, and the subsequent economic disruption will not result in anarchy and the return to a barter society. Those may have been reasonable possibilities had the same economic woes beset the world fifty or a hundred years ago when the power of central governments was relatively weak, transportation and communication slow, and man not governed by technology. Historically, debasement of a country's currency has always resulted in depression, the overthrow of the government, and anarchy if carried to the extreme. This is no longer a possibility. What is in store for the nation if the present policies continue unchecked is simply complete government ownership of the means of production; in other words, socialism. You have watched for years the gradual erosion of individual liberty and the strengthening of the power of the state. The root cause of the economic turmoil that robs you of the ability to become financially independent lies in the ever-growing federal and state bureaucracies. As the economic troubles compound, the strength of the state grows. Never has our government been stronger, and never more able to rule completely the lives of all individuals.

As the economic scenario unfolds over the next twenty years we will see an ever-increasing disruption of the productive mechanism, a gradual erosion of the standard of living of each individual, and a total collapse of the free enterprise system. As the government continues to meddle in the marketplace (i.e., wage-price controls, etc.) the devastating effects will be blamed on the inadequacy of the capitalist system to meet the needs of modern times, and the unwillingness of selfish individuals and industries to live up to their responsibilities for the welfare of the nation. The profiteering businessman will be blamed for all the ills befalling the people, and the people themselves, driven on by the propaganda mechanism of the state, will demand that the state, itself, take over control of the sagging industries. One by one they will be nationalized, either because they go bankrupt, as did Penn Central and Lockheed, or because they refuse to be responsive to the needs of the people.

We will not be destroyed by an enemy nation, we will vote ourselves into slavery.

Depression? If you define it as conditions of widespread unemployment and business failure, it will never happen. Does any communist nation suffer from unemployment? Everyone in the blissful state of socialism has a nice full time job. Of course, the standard of living falls to subsistence levels, for it is a law of nature that man will only produce efficiently when it is profitable for him to do so. When his profit is taken away and doled out to the non-producers, to the bureaucrats and welfare cases, to those too sick to work, too tired to work, too elite to work, and too crafty to work, then soon everyone will be crowding into the handout line, and only fools and slaves will produce anything.

Since the need of any corecive government is, first of all, for soldiers and guns to enforce the slavery, most of the work force and production will go directly to state needs, as it now does in most Communist or Facist countries. And if you look around you might find the United States is not too far behind these other countries in this respect. Even today one person in six is directly employed by federal, state or local government.

So to believe that the U.S. is headed for the greatest depression in its history is, by my way of thinking, foolishness. We are headed first for an ever-increasing inflation, with rates of 20%, 25% and 30% not far off. We will see an ever-increasing manipulation of business by the government. More controls, more "consumer protection," more power to the politicians. The entire regulatory mechanism of the government will smother business in megatons of paperwork, eating up the profitability of enterprise, and swelling the workforce of the bureaucracy. As businesses fall beneath the load, they will be subsidized and nationalized. Like England, we will go from a dynamic industrial giant with a standard of living the highest the world has ever known, to a whining ghost of former greatness. *Atlas Shrugged* will become a novel of prophesy.

What will the economic position of the individual be? In an economy dominated by an inflating money supply, all forces act against the interests of the producer. The direct effects of the inflation create chaotic investment markets and all the economic risks discussed in Chapter II. In addition to the speculative fever and its inherent dangers to your stored wealth, the state must survive. It has only two sources of sustenance: current production or stored wealth. It will consume both. Historically, under countries moving into the grip of socialism, the person who has any stored wealth becomes the target of the people themselves.

What can you do about the future? In regard to the state of the world today, probably very little. First educate yourself thoroughly in economics. Then set about protecting your wealth according to the principles discussed in this book. Leave the government alone. It's bigger than you and you're not going to change it. Only don't help it along by feeding it anymore than you have to.

Produce as much as you possibly can in the next few years, and store it away. Cut back, if possible, on your standard of living now, and store the excess production. Pay off your debts and mortgages, and get your assets liquid. In other words, make yourself as strong as possible financially.

You might look at the future as would a person living in a primitive agricultural society if he knew a seven year drought were coming. Rather than continue to consume his production at normal levels, he would tighten his belt and store up as much as possible for the hard years ahead. Even though this year it might seem that times were good and there was more than enough to enjoy his normal standard of living, he would be careful to conserve. Furthermore, he would realize that most people weren't bothering to store up reserves, and these people would pose threats to his stored wealth when the famine came. If he's to survive he'll need to protect that wealth. It would do him little good to try and protest the coming famine, or to get the complacent government to do anything about it. His most prudent course is simply to shut up and prepare for the future. And so is yours.

Good luck!

Appendix

MONTHLY BUDGET

	CURRENT	AFTER DEATH OF SPOUSE	IF DISABLED
REGULAR			
Mortgage or Rent			
Utilities			
Maid, Gardener, Pool Service, etc.			
Groceries, Milk, Liquor			
Lunches			
Entertainment, Meals, Shows, etc.			
Recreation (Skiing, Boating, etc.)			
Clothes			
Laundry, Cleaning, Shoe Repair			
Personal (Haircuts & Allowances)			
Auto Operation (Gas, Tires, Repairs)			
Tuitions, Lessons			
Donations			
Support of Others, Alimony, etc.			
Auto Loans (Or Amortization)			
Other Loans			
Other			
TOTAL REGULAR EXPENSES			
PERIODIC			
Real Estate Taxes			
Household Maintenance & Repair			
New Household Purchases			
Casualty Insurance (Auto, Home)			
Life Insurance			
Disability, Medical Insurance			
Vacations			
Gifts (Birthdays, Anniv., Xmas)			
Income Taxes, State & Federal			
Legal, Accounting			
Medical, Dental, Veterinarian			
Other			
TOTAL PERIODIC EXPENSES			
SAVINGS & INVESTMENTS			
Real Estate			
Securities			
Other			
TOTAL SAVINGS & INVESTMENTS			
TOTAL MONTHLY EXPENSES			

FEDERAL ESTATE TAX

Taxable Estate From:	To:	Tax Is:	Plus:	Of Amount Over:
$ 0	$ 5,000	$ 0	3%	$ 0
5,000	10,000	150	7%	5,000
10,000	20,000	500	11%	10,000
20,000	30,000	1,600	14%	20,000
30,000	40,000	3,000	18%	30,000
40,000	50,000	4,800	22%	40,000
50,000	60,000	7,000	25%	50,000
60,000	100,000	9,500	28%	60,000
100,000	250,000	20,700	30%	100,000
250,000	500,000	65,700	32%	250,000
500,000	750,000	145,700	35%	500,000
750,000	1,000,000	233,200	37%	750,000
1,000,000	1,250,000	325,700	39%	1,000,000
1,250,000	1,500,000	423,200	42%	1,250,000
1,500,000	2,000,000	528,200	45%	1,500,000
2,000,000	2,500,000	753,200	49%	2,000,000
2,500,000	3,000,000	998,200	53%	2,500,000
3,000,000	3,500,000	1,263,200	56%	3,000,000
3,500,000	4,000,000	1,543,200	59%	3,500,000
4,000,000	5,000,000	1,838,200	63%	4,000,000
5,000,000	6,000,000	2,468,200	67%	5,000,000
6,000,000	7,000,000	3,138,200	70%	6,000,000
7,000,000	8,000,000	3,838,200	73%	7,000,000
8,000,000	10,000,000	4,568,200	76%	8,000,000
10,000,000	Balance	6,088,200	77%	10,000,000

A credit is allowed against the federal estate tax, shown in the preceding table, for estate or inheritance taxes actually paid to state governments. Taxable Estate is net estate after community property division and after $60,000 personal exemption.

LIFE INSURANCE NEEDS ESTIMATE

Capital Requirements

    Debts $_____

    Income Taxes   _____

    Probate and Estate Tax   _____

    Final Expenses   _____

    Education Fund   _____

    Family Income Fund   _____

Total Capital Requirements $_____

Available Assets

    Cash $_____

    Marketable Securities   _____

    Real Estate   _____

    Business Interests   _____

    Other Assets   _____

Total Available Assets $_____

Total Life Insurance Needed $_____

PRELIMINARY ECONOMIC ANALYSIS
OF
PROFESSIONAL INCORPORATION

NET INCOME FROM SELF EMPLOYMENT   ————

ADDITIONAL CORPORATE COSTS   ————

      25% of Employees Compensation   ————

      Disability Income Premiums   ————

      Group Life Insurance Premiums   ————

      Buy-Sell Insurance Premiums   ————

      Medical Insurance Premiums   ————

      Corporate Taxes   ————

      Social Security   ————

      State Disability Income   ————

      Workemens' Compensation   ————

      Additional Accountant's Fees   ————

      Retirement Plan Trustee Fees   ————

      Total Additional Costs   ════

TOTAL AVAILABLE BEFORE RETIRE-
    MENT PLAN CONTRIBUTION   ————

RETIREMENT PLAN CONTRIBUTION
    FOR OWNER (20% of Above)   ————

BASE SALARY   ════

CORPORATE BENEFITS
VS.
SELF-EMPLOYMENT INCOME

INCORPORATED   UNINCORPORATED

INCORPORATED		UNINCORPORATED
——————	Compensation	——————
══════	Personal Exemptions, Deductions	══════
——————	Taxable Income	——————
——————	Federal Income Tax	——————
——————	State Income Tax	——————
══════	Self-Employment Tax	══════
——————	Total Taxes	——————
══════	After Tax Net (Compensation Less Taxes)	══════
	Fringe Benefits	
——————	Retirement Plan	——————
——————	Buy-Sell Life Insurance	——————
——————	Disability Insurance	——————
——————	Group Life Insurance	——————
——————	Medical Insurance	——————
——————	Total Fringe Benefits	——————
══════	After-Tax Net + Fringes	══════

References

1. Hazlitt, Henry, *Economics In One Lesson* (New York: MacFadden-Bartell Corp., 1969).

2. Browne, Harry, *How You Can Profit From The Coming Devaluation* (New Rochelle: Arlington House, 1970).

3. Hoppe, Donald J., *How To Invest In Gold Coins* (New Rochelle: Arlington House, 1970).

4. Sprinkel, Beryl Wayne, *Money & Markets: A Monetarist View* (Homewood, Ill.: Richard D. Irwin, Inc., 1971).

5. Hebling, Hans H. and Turley, James E. "A Primer on Inflation: Its Conception, Its Costs, Its Consequences", *Federal Reserve Bank of St. Louis Review* (St. Louis: Federal Reserve Bank of St. Louis, January, 1975) p. 5.

6. The Board of Governors, The Federal Reserve System, *The Federal Reserve System, Purposes And Functions* (Washington, D.C.: The Federal Reserve System).

7. McCracken, Paul W., "Fighting Inflation After Phase Two", *Fortune* (Chicago: Time, Inc., June, 1972) p. 84.

8. White, Andrew Dickson, *Fiat Money Inflation In France* (Caldwell, Idaho: The Caxton Printers, Ltd., 1972) p. 38.

9. von Mises, Ludwig, *Human Action* (New Haven: Yale University Press, 1949).

10. "The Big Headache", *Time* (Chicago: Time, Inc., September 9, 1974) p. 27.

11. Havemann, Ernest, "The Great Glut", *Life* (Chicago: Time, Inc. 1950) p. 119.

12. *U.S. News & World Report* (Washington, D.C.: U.S. News & World Report, Inc., October 9, 1972).

13.   Clason, George S., *The Richest Man In Babylon* (New York: Hawthorne Books, Inc., 1955).

14.   Swerdloff, Peter, *Money Magazine* "If It Feels Bad, It Is Bad" (Chicago: Time, Inc., November, 1973) p. 39.

15.   Hoppe, Donald J., *How To Invest In Gold Stocks And Avoid The Pitfalls* (New Rochelle: Arlington House, 1972).

16.   Burke, William and Levy, Yvonne, Silver: *End of an Era* (San Francisco: Federal Reserve Bank of San Francisco, 1972).

17.   *Understanding The Commodity Futures Market* (New York: Commodity Research Publications Co., 1973).

18.   *Federal Reserve Bulletin* (Washington, D.C.: The Federal Reserve System, July, 1974).

19.   Silveira, Antonio M. "Interest Rate and Rapid Inflation", *Journal Of Money, Credit And Banking* (Columbus: Ohio State University Press, August, 1973) p. 795.

20.   Bresciani-Turroni, Constantino, *The Economics of Inflation* (Northampton, England: Agustus M. Kelley, 1968) p. 158.

21.   Roebuck, Melvin L. and Richardson, William Alan, *Choosing A Mutual Fund For Maximum Growth* (New York: Roebuck & Co., 1970).

22.   Malkiel, Burton G., *A Random Walk Down Wall Street* (New York: W.W. Norton & Company, Inc., 1973).

23.   Sprinkel, Beryl Wayne, *Money & Stock Prices: A Monetarist View* (Homewood, Ill.: Richard D. Irwin, Inc., 1971).

24.   *College Costs* (Hartford: Life Insurance Marketing and Research Association, 1974).

25.   *A Guide To Life Insurance* (Mt. Vernon, N.Y.: Consumers Union of United States, Inc., 1974).